THE LANGUAGE OF
THE RITE

THE LANGUAGE OF THE RITE

Roger Grainger

Darton, Longman & Todd
London

First published in Great Britain in 1974 by
Darton, Longman & Todd Limited
85 Gloucester Road, London SW7 4SU

Printed in Great Britain by
Richard Clay (The Chaucer Press) Ltd,
Bungay, Suffolk

ISBN 0 232 51246 9

Contents

5-16-78

In Memory of
Robert Lambourne

Foreword

Before the most recent spate of liturgical reform believers had the privilege of saying: 'It is very meet, right and our bounden duty that we should at all times and all places give thanks unto Thee, almighty Father, holy and everlasting God.' Ritual is about those things which are very meet, right, and our bounden duty. It concerns what is Rite and Proper, Right and Appropriate. There is an element of meeting, of bond and of duty. But is the bond 'merely' the social bond and is the duty 'merely' the pressure of society indirectly transmitted? Durkheim thought that it was, and in the course of magnifying religion as the source of social bonding he diminished it as a mere emanation of man's communal awareness.

In this book, Mr Grainger maintains that Durkheim committed an exciting tautology and a pregnant mistake. Religion, we can say (with John Wesley), is at least social: the most inadequate characterisation of religion is 'The Flight of the alone to the Alone'. It is also more because it is a language translatable only in its own terms, concerned with initiation into new possibilities, with a death and a meeting. It alters by reference to the *Alter*. It speaks in figures which are trans-figured. And speaking in this unique way it is not susceptible to reduction: its logic, structure, and referents are its own. At this point I become uncertain, since the language of religion certainly appears to overlap other languages and one is unhappy about just how far language-games are hermetically sealed off, one from another.

Let me illustrate the code, which whether sealed off from other codes or not, can represent a logical structure of immense power and coherence. As we recite the Creed we say ... *et incarnatus est de Spiritu Sancto ex Maria Virgine et homo factus est.* What does this mean? It means that the continuities of human culture transmitted through families from generation to generation have been radically broken. It means that Spirit makes an incursion into all the recalcitrant inertias of culture which inserts a divine possibility. It also means that such a possibility is constricted within the limits of human social activity. The divine possibility is embodied and 'contained', constricted by the body of a man and the rules of the body of society. The power of this incursion must take account of the powers that be. Ritual, above all the Eucharist, is the continuing expression of that embodiment: the body of a man given to the social body. Here, there is a clear distinction of languages. The 'body' in the language of religion is not the same as the body in the language of biology. Similarly when we used to say according to the old use that the 'property of God is always to have mercy', the distinction between 'property' as predicated of God and physical objects is quite clear. But the 'power' of God at least has *relationships* with the powers that be. The language of religion has complex connections with the language of society. When this book explores the language of ritual I also wish it were able fully to explore these connections.

But it does show us what the structure and language of a rite is. It shows us what kind of signals, including transcendent signals, are transmitted in the rite in order to put us 'in the right'. It shows the positive and the negative elements: the green signals and the red. If our liturgical signalmen are indeed colour blind, as Professor Mary Douglas has claimed, then this book would help them to understand the 'bricolage' with which they are dealing. Indeed, all those who have been stimulated by Professor Mary Douglas' discussions of ritual and boundaries, whether students of anthropology or religion, should enjoy the discussion carried forward here.

DAVID MARTIN
Professor of Sociology in the University of London
at The London School of Economics and Political Science

Introduction

What is the rite? It is religious aspiration which has been given the form of corporate art. It is a special kind of language for speaking about God and men. Because it uses actual men and women, their bodies, minds, and imaginations to do so, it is able to be particularly frank and precise about human things, the characteristics, powers and limitations of men. For the very same reason it is able to be explicit about religion; that is, about the *difference* between men and the gods they worship. But whether or not men are consciously motivated by religion, they still need the rite for the experience of communion. The same honesty that marks the ritual approach to God allows people to 'be themselves' in the presence of one another. In the rite, a man 'acts out with his body what he thinks out with his brain.'[1] He uses the language of demonstration; and what he demonstrates is a real meeting of persons in which emotions, thoughts, attitudes, the experience of life itself, can all be shared.

The rite, then, 'corresponds to a basic human need', the need for a kind of self-expression which does not merely involve the mind but includes the whole person, and which is not rebuffed by the presence of others, but receives the gift of that presence for the free bestowal of itself. This fact was better understood and

[1] Eric Fromm, 'The Sane Society', Routledge, 1956.

more widely accepted in former ages and other civilisations than the present. In classical times in particular, ritual contributed powerfully to the business of everyday living, and 'fundamental problems of human existence were presented in an artistic and dramatic form' (Eric Fromm). This was the theatre of audience participation, the drama that attained the force and intensity of corporate ritual. We have largely lost sight of it. Our experiments in this direction have been confined to theatre buildings, for the benefit of a socially and intellectually exclusive 'theatre public'. The stuff of corporate awareness, as this concerns the individual at the deepest and most personal level, has become a minority interest, a footnote to society. The common food of social belonging has become 'caviare to the general'. Theatre and sacramental religion have both been largely rejected by modern Western society. The result is that society finds itself without adequate channels of inter-personal communication and corporate experience. The results are to be found in the lives of individuals. As one contemporary commentator has it, 'it seems likely that one dimension of mental illness may arise because an increasing number of individuals are forced to accomplish their transitions (that is, the crises of their development as persons) alone, and with their private symbols' S. Kimball, 1960).

The corporate rite has suffered attacks from various directions. The most persistent assaults have been those delivered by theology itself, psychopathology, and anthropology. In the following pages we shall be examining some of these attacks and commenting on their validity. The rejection of ritual is no isolated phenomenon. The rite is a structure. It employs a certain number of fixed actions, each one of which transmits a single, more or less definite meaning. Change the actions, or the order of the actions, and the rite's meaning is completely changed. Nowadays there is a tendency to regard all structures with the deepest suspicion. Structure itself is considered to be the enemy of freedom and spontaneity. Relationship, the truth of human meeting, has no need of structure.

This however, is a view that seems, to say the least, extremely suspect. Indeed we completely reject it. We maintain instead that freedom and spontaneity *emerge from* structure. Structure inhibits relationships, or intrudes between persons, only when it is not understood and acknowledged. That society can no more dispense with structures than men can go about without their bodies is a truism. But it is not only necessary to have them it is essential that we should accept the fact that we rely upon them. Only thus can our ideas about human relationships be free from self-delusion, and our pronouncements about ourselves be honest accounts of the facts.

Ritual is a statement about man's identity as structured spirit. In the rite man stands forth in all his limited and conditioned freedom, as the embodied soul, separated and defined, given individuality, by his own body, living in relation to others who are at once like and unlike himself, whom he knows as his fellows and meets as strangers. The contradiction must be preserved. It is essential to our understanding of human relationship. For it is from this tension of self and other, sameness and difference, that personality arises. The structure of the rite allows the interaction of persons who are both interdependent and independent, and neither isolated nor confused.

Because it is concerned with this tension between individuals, ritual is about community. For community is about freedom. Paradoxical as it may seem, the unity of mankind depends upon what keeps people apart. It is the obstacle of differentiation, the division into selves, which permits the movement of relation, the soul's outgoing gesture. Upon this movement, this gesture, society really stands. Social influences and pressures, incumbent upon us all, may govern our behaviour as people: but without a certain inalienable uniqueness, literal and symbolic, we are not people at all.

As our awareness of inter-existence and interdependence increases, our need for modes of communication and self-expression which preserve the truth of personal identity grows ever more urgent. Twentieth-century social man, more anxious than ever to define the terms of his own freedom in an arbitrary world, must somehow re-discover the ancient language of ritual, which is able to speak the unlimited, unconditioned possibility of Spirit, at the same time as it acknowledges the various determinisms of the flesh.

1 The Language of Ritual

1. Religion and Societies

People have mixed feelings about rituals. They object to them in theory, sometimes quite strongly. And yet they welcome the opportunity to take part in them. A wedding attracts a crowd, and so, in a different way, does a funeral. The appeal is there, there is no doubt about it; we might call it the appeal of a corporate celebration, the drawing-power of a licensed emotional release. We linger a few moments at the church door as the bride emerges; we are tempted to take up a handful of confetti and join in. It is the same at baptisms; we may not understand the real significance of the font, its primeval message of death and re-birth, but we know that we like it when the Parson kisses the baby, and makes an ordinary action 'part of the service'.

As to secret rituals – the heavily guarded initiatory rites which go along with becoming a mason or a Buffalo (or even, in some cases, a full member of the church choir!), or the terrifying mysteries which hedge in the privileged camaraderie of American university fraternities like an electric fence around some paradisal holiday-camp – their fascination is profound and timeless.

Really timeless; in some strange way, these 'protected' or privileged rites have managed to resist time, to survive the many pressures of modern society, pressures at one and the same time unifying and fragmenting, in that they disrupt traditional cultural groupings while reducing communities to an undifferentiated traditional sameness of isolated family groupings. There is evidence to show that the need to belong to a specialised group, club, or society is intensified rather than lessened by the pressures of standardisation and the tendency towards uniformity of habits and attitudes. In the sphere of religion, sects proliferate as denominations decline in numbers and popularity, and hence in drawing power. With the emergence of the pluralist society (philosophically and culturally pluralist) which is genuinely secular in its beliefs, the religious awareness, where this can really be said to exist within society, has become more, and not less, intense. To a certain extent, the old saying, that 'the blood of the martyrs is the seed of the Church' remains true. Those seeking ordination within the older-established denominations have a sense of personal involvement, an almost desperate commitment, that a previous generation would have found strange and perhaps a little alarming. People conform less and choose more; religious belonging, where it exists, is at a deeper and more personal level.

But the appeal of religious ritual is not only to the initiate. The ordinary public rituals of the church attract because of their usefulness. The ceremonies which, to the committed believer, possess real religious authority and value, perform a traditional role in giving stability and form to society itself. It is worth remembering (indeed, it is a fact that lies at the root of any adequate explanation of religious ritual) that an act of corporate symbolism is an act of power; of real human power, in a basic anthropological sense. It affects all who take part in it at a fundamental level, a level much deeper and more profound than the satisfaction which comes from expressing shared emotions or proclaiming a common philosophy or ideology. The act itself expresses and asserts social solidarity and belonging, whatever it is used for. The terms in which it proposes to embody that solidarity, the reasons it gives for it – what we might call the 'mythology' of solidarity – may be secondary.

In contemporary Western society they are usually so. Indeed, many people are accustomed to thinking of religion not as something to join or belong to, but as a way of giving a metaphysical dimension to events or happenings in their lives which they hold to be specially important. Religion is a way of giving these events a certain depth and significance, of assuring their registration within the public and private consciousness as valid happenings. It is important, for example, that birth and death should be *somebody*'s birth and *somebody*'s death; that they should, to use Kathleen Bliss's[1] term, be 'namings'; and that 'the community should have better ways of doing honour to persons than reporting their names in the registrar's records'. Religious rites, being both dignified and traditional, present themselves as specially appropriate for the purpose of establishing the personal by affording it public recognition. Thus religion lends public dignity to private occasions. It performs a useful service in setting up land-marks and establishing boundaries. It says things as if they were important. For a lot of people, that is enough.

In fact, however, there is much more than this. What really happens in the rite is both more honest and more complicated. Nothing is 'lent' to an occasion at all by the rite; but something is revealed. The rite's dignity is not borrowed for the occasion. Quite the opposite. As anyone who has attended a baptism, a wedding, or a funeral in church knows (and which of us has not? 70 per cent of marriages, and all baptisms and funerals take place in a religious setting) the occasion is dignified by the innate significance of the rite itself, its inalienable importance to the central actor or actors and the supporting cast of relatives and friends. Actions and observances undertaken lightly enough, often in a spirit of amused agnosticism, penetrate deeply and leave their mark. This is not merely the satisfaction of having performed a prescribed social ritual and registered

3

one's status as a member of society in a formal way. This is not any kind of 'formality', but an act of power, an act which draws its power from its ability to assert and establish the integrity of primal human belonging, the integrity of the human race as a whole. These ordinary ceremonies of the church are able to change reality in a special way, a way that defies analysis. They are concerned, not to describe reality, but to expand it beyond description; they are ways of accommodating, within our experience of present limitation, our measurable finitude, a practical vision of perfection. In other words, they are what we knew them to be all along, but had conveniently forgotten – *religious* acts.

The claim, then, is this. That the ceremonies of the Church are acts of religious power; that this is the real nature of their appeal to us; that those who are drawn to them are drawn for genuinely religious reasons, and those who reject them do so for the same reasons. It is the sheer power of the rite that gives rise to the ambivalence, the rather shame-faced fascination which we have remarked on. We may say that a real fear, produced by the consciousness of powerful forces which are unacknowledged, looks for, and finds, theoretical objections to consorting with such forces, to entering the Holy Place. We shall attempt to answer these objections later on. For the time being it must be pointed out that equally theoretical arguments are offered in defence of ritual by those who find its mana irresistible. The truth is that ritual is not an adjunct of religion, to be either defended or opposed. In a real sense, it *is* religion.

The connection between religion in general and specific religious rites is a very close one. The rite is the very core of religious awareness – its reality, its heart, its truthfulness in tangible shape. All religions have rites, just as they all possess theologies. If we find the latter proposition more easy to accept than the former, this is because of the relative simplicity and spontaneity of some religious ritual behaviour, which makes us hesitate to call its observance rites. However it is possible (as Hegel noted with regard to Hamlet) for inaction itself to be a form of action; and this is particularly so about behaviour in the presence of Divinity. The quiet informality of a Quaker meeting-house constitutes the Friends' ritual expression of their feeling about God and themselves. Their *ritual* expression; for this is how they always behave in the meeting. It would be quite improper to behave otherwise. All religions have rites. Some, we are led to believe, only have rites, in the sense that their worship is wordless, or almost wordless.[1] There is no need for a man's relation to God to be over-burdened with words, or for his thinking about God to be as developed and involved as S. Thomas's. And so a worshipper's chief act of devotion – the reality of his or her religion – may be to light a lamp at a shrine, to lay a garland of flowers in the mouth of a cave; to dance, to process, to re-enact a wordless salvation–history, a drama which may be simple or involved, but which needs no spoken commentary. Indeed, words would be considered to be superfluous; they would simply get in the way.

What historians of religion call 'developed religions', the Greek and Roman Mysteries, Buddhism, Hinduism, Christianity, possess involved scenarios in order to embody, and to demonstrate, their understanding of the relationship of man with God, and man with his fellows, and to underline their special awareness of the vital significance of that relationship. The religious rituals of the Kurnai of Western Australia, on the other hand, or of the Yamaha of Tierra del Fuego, are extremely simple. But in both cases, where religion is 'developed' and where it remains 'un-developed', the rites are there, and are quite inseparable from the thinking enshrined within them. To try and separate the words of religious acts from the acts themselves is a pointless exercise. The words of the rite are the result of reflection. The actions, however, reveal a need to express understanding or awareness of a different kind – the urge towards immediate response to a reality which is specifically religious. This is non-propositional, precognitive, instinctive. When we get down to examining the basic nature of religious phenomena we find that action precedes word, and not word action.

Religion originates in the instinctive movement of response to Divinity. It develops into a partnership of action and word, for the experienced truth of the theology expressed, its acceptance by, and incorporation within, the understanding, completes this instinctive, non-thetic movement on the part of the worshipper. But the theology must itself be more than simply theoretical, more than a plausible explanation. It must be capable of becoming part of the life of the worshipper, part of his very flesh and blood and bones. It must not only make sense, it must make the *right kind of sense*. The story itself must awaken experiential memories, arouse emotional echoes, within us. The theology of our religions proceeds, not from reflection upon the evidence presented by the immediate reality–situation, but from the assimilation of experience, both individual and corporate.

Christians will see the relevance of these remarks. However, they are not only applicable to the Christian religion, but to religion in general, religions throughout the world. For religion is an existential phenomenon, not a philosophy. As such, it is generalised and universal, belonging to nature rather than to culture. The truth of the matter is that religious philosophies and theologies are cultural phenomena, and exist in different forms in different societies, or even in varying forms within the same society. Religion itself, however, is a different kind of thing altogether. It exists wherever men exist. Social anthropologists refer to it as a social phenomenon, historians of religion as a natural expression of being human. It would certainly be foolish to dwell on this distinction, for the obvious reason that man is a social animal. The existence of religion as a social fact is not disputed by anthropologists.

However, it should be stated that, in the opinion of some modern writers – notably, Claude Levi-Strauss,[2] Professor Evans-Pritchard,[3] and, latterly, Mary Douglas[4] – the relationship between society and religion has been dangerously misunderstood. It has been misunderstood, say these writers, at the expense of the status of religion as an expression of society, a natural, inalienable, social characteristic. Attacks have been mounted on two main fronts. First of all, it has been the practice among social anthropologists to attempt an explanation of particular religions in terms of particular societies; and so to regard a particular religion as existing in order to perform a useful function with regard to maintaining the stability of the culture it has been evolved to serve – in other words, to bestow a divine blessing on, or provide a metaphysical explanation for the civil status-quo in a particular place at a particular time. Religion and society being co-terminous, the former may be interpreted and understood according to the logic which holds good with regard to the latter. Since the beginning of depth-psychology, the favourite functional, or psychological, explanation of religious behaviour has definitely been the Freudian[5] one, conveniently expanded to take account of nations as well as individuals.

Of these two 'explanations', the first commends itself by taking account of the corporate nature of religious belonging. Indeed, the religious rite affords an ideal field of operation for social anthropologists because it is, essentially, an expression of corporateness. A rite is a society; and where religion is universally accepted, the rite is *the* society. It simply cannot be explained in terms of the psychological economy of individuals. At least, as Evans-Pritchard[3] points out, it cannot be explained in such terms within the discipline of Social Anthropology, which sees societies in terms of what they display openly in their social groupings, not in what they reveal hesitantly and often unwillingly on the psychiatrist's couch. But the first explanation is not really much more satisfactory, and seems to ask more questions than it is able to answer. If the function of religion is simply to give plausibility to societies, to make them more credible to their members, why is it that those members hold their religion to be so much more important, at the deepest level, than the society which it serves? Why, if it be held that society precedes religion, is a society's worth explained in religious terms, as an image of a greater and more valuable reality? Surely the logical thing would be simply to worship the state itself; but state-worship, the dedication of Divinity to the service of civil authority, is universally accepted as the mark of debased and de-vitalised religions, which are hardly religions at all. Why – and this is an even more troublesome question – is religion itself not more credible? Why does one society, for example, pay homage to a transcendent spiritual being who is totally unlike men, but demands their painful participation in his own value-system, while another rejoices in a whole pantheon of divinities whose behaviour is all too human, and seems, at first sight, to infringe every moral law acknowledged by the society whose exemplars they are supposed to be? Why, indeed, are there so many religions, and all so different from one another? Anthropologists point out that the number of religious systems is very considerably greater than the recorded variations among social structures. And – the final question – what about societies which worship, not Gods or Heroes, but birds, beasts, and fishes? In other words, what has social anthropology to say about the 'problem' of totemism? After all, it is the notion that religion is explicable in terms of the nature and needs of human social organisation that makes the worship of non-human creatures into a 'problem' in the first place: just how is this problem to be solved?

2. *Levi-Strauss*[2] *and the Diversification of Cultures*

Why do particular tribal groupings attach a religious significance and value to certain non-human creatures; and what lies behind the choice of a particular creature by a particular tribe or nation? The answer to this question may provide us with the clue to all the others we have been asking. There are two obvious answers, neither of which is very satisfactory. The first, which we might call the 'functionalist' answer, as it is associated with the followers of Malinowski,[6] is that the particular creature performs a vital function within the society concerned. This function may be positive or negative – the creature may be useful or it may be terrifying – but its function is always a *literal* one. The second, or Durkheimian,[6] explanation is more authentically sociological rather than psychological. The chosen creature is venerated as a symbol, or as part of a symbol, of society itself. Society thus worships itself, under the forms of the behaviour of birds, fishes, animals. But why does it choose a particular animal or bird? Why that particular one? It is because of the terrifying number of variations among the totems chosen and the apparent illogicality of their choice as emblems and objects of worship that the anthropologist Claude Levi-Strauss has been led to reject the idea of religion as a function of society; as a function, that is, of a particular society, explicable in terms of the society which professes it. The questions anthropologists are accustomed to ask about religion, the questions we were asking in the previous section, cannot be answered, says Levi-Strauss, because they are not real questions. They do not represent real problems. The clue to our understanding of the matter is to be found, not in the agreement, or lack of agreement, between a society and its religion *looked at as if societies and religions were the same kind of thing and could be compared*, but in the consistency and articulation of a particular religion, and its relation to the consistency and the articulation achieved or sought after within a particular social grouping. A totemic system does not come into existence because of a relationship between its principals, be they sacred personages or sacred animals, fishes, birds, etc., and the men and women in a community, which is regarded as significant, but because of a relationship existing, or considered to exist, among the principals themselves, which is held to have a religious meaning and value for human society. Human societies, it is believed, should aspire to a similar relatedness and co-ordination, and ought to think of themselves in terms of such modes of organisation as exist within the totem; ought, in other words, to think of themselves in an *ideal* way. Thus, totemism and the worship of Gods and heroes are part of the same phenomenon; they are a way of thinking which tends towards the improvement of society by bringing it into line with nature seen as a consistent whole, that is, with ideal nature, or with super-nature.

The key to all this is to be found in linguistics. For a religion is a kind of language. It is built up out of similarities and oppositions, as human thought, and consequently human communication, expresses itself dialectically and analogically. It obeys its own rules, as language does, and can be translated only as a whole if it is to make complete sense. A French grammatical construction, for instance, will make nonsense of an English sentence, and vice versa. But the whole sentence may be translated from one language to the other without loss of meaning. Again, languages are parallel, but not necessarily interchangeable. We use a different kind of language when we want to express a different quality of experience. The language of poetry is not the same as the language of mathematics. Similarly, the language of religion runs parallel to that of society and social concepts; the one sheds light upon the other, but is most unsatisfactory as an explanation of it. For practical purposes of comparison and analysis, the language of religion is incomplete and often inconsistent; it seems a clumsy tool to use in describing any existent society.

From another view-point, however, the language of religion, the code of taboo, is perfectly adequate. For the religious code is constructed and articulated in order to express ideas and experiences which lie outside the range of the social language, while remaining in the closest relation to that language. The language of the rite is intended to express a dimension of being which is more consistent and more complete than the social one, the dimension of religious experience. These two languages are not intended to be completely interchangeable; in fact, they are kept different on purpose. The grammar of ritual is the relationship of personages within the rite itself. Because it makes use of living personages, whether these are human or non-human, ritual is always a language about society, an existential language about the experience of relationship, rather than a language for the transmission of ideas in the abstract. But its difference from society *as it exists* is more important than its similarity to it. The cast of characters in the rite are not intended to be like people as we know them in ordinary life, the world of the rite is not intended to be like our world, but to demonstrate a more perfect way of being, an improved world of better relationships. This is a better world, these are better people. This is not to say that the choice of taboo 'personages' is entirely arbitrary and that any animal or bird will be considered appropriate as a symbol of corporate excellence. The 'functionalist' writers are surely right when they draw attention to a relationship between a society and its taboo which depends upon a certain basic reasonableness. Agrarian societies are likely to worship hero-figures, masters and mistresses of the sun and the moon, the earth and the seasons; hunting communities will choose to talk in ritual terms of beasts and birds and fishes.[7] But the ritual relationship, the *religious* relationship, does not depend on this kind of logic, and only makes use of the notion of likelihood to stress the presence of the *un*likely. Ritual uses homogeneity and sameness to demonstrate *difference*. It starts out from ideas and experiences which 'fit', and carries us into the new, the strange, the 'unfit', which has the power radically to transform our previous notions of fitness. The functionalist explanation of taboo systems depends on the ritual code reproducing the dominant attitudes towards, and expectations of, the environment, which hold good in a particular community; society and its code of belief about the world are mutually explanatory. The *structuralist* expectation of such systems is that there will not be a 'one-to-one' correspondence, but the religious code will be an attempt at restructuring society with a view to achieving a desired eventual correspondence, an 'ideal fit', in the future. The religious society envisaged and presented in the rite bears no straightforward or naturalistic resemblance either to existing societies or even to the life of the animals who may provide the symbolic language of the rite. In other words, these animals, fishes, birds, etc., are actors in a play which those taking part do not intend to be realistic, in any limiting sense of the word – which is why animals and not people are chosen for the parts.

As with the characters in the rite, so with the rite itself, its purpose and effect. The rite's purpose is not simply to express religious feelings and ideas which already exist in society, and thus re-state what is already known, but to create a tension out of which some new knowledge, some deeper and more intense understanding, can proceed. It is a laboratory, a melting-pot, an arena; which is why so many rites are stylised battles of some kind or another. The basic tension is always clear enough : it is between things as they are and things as they should be. The outcome is not always shown as a straightforward victory for the representatives of positive goodness; indeed, the conflict is sometimes confused, and the attitude of those taking part ambivalent. But at least the battle has been fought. And something is changed.

The tension is relieved in the actual performance of the rite. In the rite reality and aspiration are synthesised, and the result is a new quality of reality. The acting-out of idealism alters our experience of life in the ordinary, commonplace world of every day. Once expressed in concrete terms, the metaphysical perfection that we seek seems contagious. Just as, in spoken language, our choice of words has an effect upon the actual experience we are describing, limiting and defining it, setting it alongside other experiences – so the language of ritual comments on its own message. 'The rite does not merely express, it modifies.'[4] It does not simply externalise experience, it actually creates it. In Chapter 4 we shall examine how it manages to do this.

3. *Eliade and the Homology of Rites*

We may say that the principal mistake of earlier anthropologists was the confusion of religion itself with specific religions, the confusion of a primary irreducible phenomenon with its individual expressions, its particular choice of symbols in any specific society. No doubt there is a connection between society and religion. But this connection cannot be used to explain the similarities and differences of particular religions, or to shed light on a particular society's way of embodying its own religious awareness. To talk about 'social man' and 'religious man' is to use two different ideas, which are at the same time equally valid, without being at all interchangeable. They are 'same-level' ideas; the one may not simply be reduced to the other. The question of the relationship between religion and society emerges as an epistemological question, a matter of the way in which we *know* and express to ourselves our knowing. The religious person, and the student of religions, are prepared to know differently from the social scientist; they attribute value to different sorts of happenings, ideas, experiences. They see the world differently. And the same is true of the psychologist or the biologist. It is possible to know religiously, sociologically, psychopathologically, politically, and as many other ways as there are world-views; and all these 'ways of knowing' have existential value.

Persistently, the social anthropologist has been content to explain religious phenomena in terms of social organisation; either the two are identical (in the sense that the first is a simple expression of the second), or the first justifies its separate identity by its services to the second. The first of these two kinds of attitude is typified by Robertson Smith and Durkheim ('The God of the Clan ... can be nothing else than the Clan itself'; *The Elementary Forms of the Religious Life*). The second finds its clearest expression in the work of Bronislaw Malinowski, to whom religion is principally a way of reinforcing present social custom by reference to the sanctity of the past. Religion is 'a pragmatic charter of primitive faith and moral wisdom – a narrative resurrection of a primeval reality, told in satisfaction of deep religious wants, moral cravings, and social submissions, assertions, even practical requirements'.

Myth and ritual are the ways in which society reassures itself: they bolster society up. They are voices out of the past, part of a cultural heritage. This is why they exist.

Perhaps it is a little unfair to expect anthropologists to acknowledge the presence within culture itself of forces or influences of a supra-cultural nature, which lie outside the terms of reference provided by social systems, and which may themselves be held to constitute the specific terms of reference of those systems! But even Malinowski calls attention to 'the creative acts of religion', and states quite clearly that religion contributes something of its own to societies in terms of inherited sanctity and 'survival value' for the future. This does not come from the organisation of social institutions for practical purposes of survival, but from 'the tension of instinctive need', which 'leads *in some way or other* to cult and belief'. Surely this may be held to imply some kind of autonomous religious instinct, at least insofar as this is a movement of aspiration? What we might call the human aspect of religion begins to emerge as something qualitatively different from other kinds of human experience, either social or personal.

Religion, then, is becoming accepted more and more as an irreducible phenomenon, a true *chose en soi*. It is not to be explained, but must be allowed to explain itself. Like every self-consistent language, it transmits its messages by means of homology rather than by analogy, expressing itself in terms of its own manufacture, without any direct reference to other languages. 'Holiness systems', like scientific propositions, are given aesthetic shape, so that they form complexes of balanced meanings, expressive of certain distinct kinds of experience, parallel but not completely interchangeable. If religion borrows, it is in order to transform what it borrows into itself: it can be translated into something else only at the cost of losing something of its own vital and individual nature in the translation. There is no word for God, or faith, or sanctification, in the code of mathematics, or psychology, or sociology, any more than there is the possibility of precise measurement in the language of ritual and theology; and we are left with the usual analogies, the inevitable attempt to make do with something approximate, which turns out to be fatally inaccurate. And yet these are all real existential facts. As such they deserve to be expressed. Indeed, if our understanding, our *record*, of human life is to be an authentic one, it is essential to express them.

But this is the whole point of having separate codes. To understand religion in a non-religious way, to express it in non-religious language (that is, in language which is genuinely non-religious, and not just in secular terms which are intended to carry religious significance, 'new words for old meanings') is inevitably to reduce it.

The word 'reduce' is used here quite literally. Religion raises phenomena to a parity of value with itself and its objects. It postulates a divinised experience. All religions assert that men are potentially divine. There is, in religion, a homology of ultimate truth. Religious explanations exist because explanations in terms of the world of everyday, the essentially *compromised* world of human social and personal 'arrangements for survival', are found to be both inappropriate and inadequate within the sphere of the divine. The explanations offered by religion are always symbols; in other words, they exist within the religious code itself. They *are* that code. Religious explanations do not explain one thing in terms of something else, something *other*, as scientific explanations do; they do not establish the explanation at the cost of the thing explained, reducing the thing experienced to the method of organising our experience of it. As we have said, they are homological and not analogical, moving 'sideways within the system' rather than 'upwards' into another thought-system in a way that de-values the first in order to establish the second. Indeed they cannot do so, for the religious code must *by definition* be the 'highest' code of all. Symbols are never adequately explained; adequately, that is, in the scientific sense. They always remain symbols of that which defies explanation. It is science in its many forms that reduces them to signs, pointing away from their own world, their own truth, in order to 'explain' that world and that truth. Pointing away so successfully, indeed, that the original truth, the distinctively religious truth of mankind's primal vision, is completely lost.

It would be true to say that the symbols of religion function in precisely the opposite way to the signs used by science. Because they are symbols they lift us up into a new reality which is more than a shorthand expression of our present reality, pointing onwards and upwards in a religious sense towards a deeper and more real religious experience, a profounder religious knowledge, a greater sense of religious identity – all inexplicable concepts in scientific terms, and inaccessible, in their fulness, to psychopathology. Religious language speaks of men and Gods within a shared context of belonging. However exalted may be his doctrine of divinity, the believer still thinks it feasible to talk about the reality of life in the world and the possibility, or even the presence of an unseen reality, a *divine* reality, in the same sentence, in the same breath even. The existence of religious language, the existence of theology, leads him into the use of homology to express his experience in ways which remain nonsensical to the religious outsider. But it lifts him up and gives him courage and hope even to talk and think of such things.

The purpose of the religious code, then, is not to explain but to exalt; to lift a man up and to endow his world with a deeper truth and a wider meaning. Reductionism is out of the question here. We are dealing with an autonomous and self-authenticating experiential fact, encoded within a consistent language, the language of theology and mythology, which not only eschews naturalistic explanations, but evades them as basically inappropriate and un-expressive. A myth or a doctrine may, in its details, bear witness to the psychology of the human being who selected the appropriate symbols to be used in its construction (what Levi-Strauss calls the rite's 'bricologe'), but its conception, character, and purpose, its 'dramatis personae', its scenario[1] itself – in fact, its specific *language* – reveal an ideal logic, a perfect reasonableness, a sense of the basic and primary fitness of things, that belongs, not to the ideas and experiences of one man, or even of one community, but to religion itself, religion as a universal phenomenon.

Writing from different view-points, and representing the separate disciplines of Social Anthropology and the History of Religion, Professor Evans-Pritchard[3] and Claude Levi-Strauss[2] for anthropology, and Mary Douglas,[4] Robert Graves,[8] and Mircea Eliade[7] for religion, agree that religion is an autonomous phenomenon, something which can be compared with other phenomena for the purpose of explaining human experience and behaviour, but not something which can be explained in terms of other phenomena; not something which can be explained *away*. Theologians would, of course, wholeheartedly agree with this judgement. They would say that religious ideas differ in quality from the ideas encoded in other thought-systems: that such ideas are essentially doctrines – that is, that they are teachings which proceed from a shared experience which may or may not owe their authority to the laws of scientific logic. In much the same way, Eliade isolates religious thought from other kinds of philosophy by stressing its ideological nature, its power to transmute human life. But the 'argument from anthropology' is a powerful one, too. Cultures are demonstrated by Levi-Strauss, and before him by Radcliffe-Brown, to be self-contained systems, understandable only in their own terms, whose meaning abides in their wholeness and resists fragmentation. Religions, with their specific theologies, mythologies, languages, are themselves examples of distinctive cultures. They can only be satisfactorily explained as being themselves explanations, or attempts at explanation-blueprints for an idealised reality. Strictly 'practical' explanations of religion do not work out, because the system

---

[1] 'Scenario' here means the plot of the rite. It signifies the dynamic inter-relation of particular actions or separate ceremonies, their particular meaning within the context of the whole rite. 'Scenario' is the rite's acted message, which is apparent only in its entirety.

does not fit the fact. Objects, creatures, people, divine or semi-divine are worshipped for no obvious reason; that is, for no utilitarian or functional reason. Useful objects and powerful forces are not worshipped at all, although they may be respected in a practical sense, for practical reasons. Totemism turns out to be genuine religion, and not a kind of primitive domestic hygiene, an attempt to cope with the practical needs of living by inculcating fear and respect for a hostile or untrustworthy environment. It is genuine religion because it is 'predictive and evaluative'. Indeed, it is only in such terms that it is to be understood at all, for it depends upon a reality which it itself posits, and which functions according to its own logic. Self-consistent thought-systems and codes of behaviour express the fact of *religion* – which we might describe as 'relationship to Significant Otherness', the mystical, open-ended, search for transcendent value – in terms of specific *religions*. Religion speaks, not its own language, but its own languages. These are formulated to express aspirations, ideals, and transformations, rather than to present reality in any restrictive, 'scientific', or non-religious sense, reality untouched by religious awareness. They are all different, as the cultures in which they evolve are all different. After all, it was in order to 'speak to' a specific culture that they were contrived in the first place, so we should not be surprised if they possess features which are unique to that culture. Indeed, we may say that the culture itself was shaped and moulded by its religious beliefs; and this is why those beliefs cannot be reduced to anything which is itself non-religious. It is impossible to explain the thing that leads in terms of that which follows.[2]

[2] 'Both psychologists and historians of religion have come to renounce explanations of the origins of religion that would reduce it to something in man that is not itself religious. The primitive and irreducible character of religion as a social fact and individual experience is all the more manifest today in that we can now describe more accurately the roots it has in human nature' – Bouyer.[9] Since Schliermacher, theology has largely abandoned the attempt to justify itself in non-religious terms. Science has not been so generous; it has taken sociologically-orientated writers such as Evans-Pritchard to point out the basically un-scientific nature of attempts to regard

We have made use of the notion of languages and codes which are separate and autonomous in order to avoid the tendency towards the common practice of explaining, or seeming to explain, a phenomenon by talking about it in language appropriate to something else. A phenomenon so diverse and yet so consistent must, we have said, be simply *itself*. Religions can be explained and understood only in terms of religion. Being of primary status, they are otherwise inexplicable. But in order to do this we have been forced into the somewhat invidious position of seeming to endanger the credibility of religion itself. For we have had to draw attention to the very thing that appears to stand in the way of its acceptance as an irreducible factual reality. This is the sheer number of different religions, the proliferation of theologies and credal systems, which is so often used to attack the institution of religion itself. But the number and variety of religions is governed by the number and variety of cultures, rather than by any real element of choice with regard to the basic nature of religion. Religion itself, the search for a higher mode of existence, for a life which transcends the limitations of non-religious reality, must make use of a code which has been specially designed for it, specially designed to reveal its uniqueness as an experiential phenomenon – but such a code will always bear witness to the special circumstances of that experience, its geographical location and historical, or supra-historical time-scale. Indeed, it is difficult to see how it could be otherwise. The cultural expression of religion differs. But religion remains itself. And the proof lies in the rite.

Culture and society are not to be taken as congruent entities. There are many cultures, and only a limited number of permutations among social systems. What *is* consistent, however, is that culture is the language of aspiration, whatever vocabulary may be used. And something else is consistent too – the basic, underlying framework of religious languages and codes stays un-

---

one discipline as if it were another: 'we don't study engineering as if it were biology, or biology as if it were engineering'.

changed throughout the world; or, at least, the structures of
religious behaviour maintain everywhere a peculiar consistency
and uniformity. Theologies differ, but rites remain the same.
On one level, the rite represents the grammatical sub-structure,
the system of contrasts and similarities, dissonances and resolu-
tions, without which language itself cannot exist as a way of
codifying experience, and which characterises all languages,
and every code of communication.

But we may go further than this. A language needs grammatical rules. Because they depend upon the initial juxtaposition
of positive and negative elements, these rules are bound, to
some extent, to resemble one another. But a comparison of
religions throughout the world reveals that, at the level of basic
religious ritual, the resemblance is much closer than this. The
grammar of corporate religion, the morphology or outline of
the rite, tends everywhere to reproduce itself. In this sense, the
rite is the rock upon which all public religion is based. The
primal religious scenario is, in fact, that drama of re-birth, of
religious self-transcendence, to which we have drawn attention;
it is the initiation rite, analysed structurally by van Gennep,[10]
and traced throughout the majority of the world's religions by
Mircea Eliade. Indeed, Eliade argues that this particular way of
expressing religious beliefs and feelings is fundamental to the
human consciousness. Initiation may be of an entire age range
within a certain society, as in puberty rituals; of an élite, as in
initiation into secret societies of various degrees and kinds of
secrecy; or of an individual, as in the making of priests or
shamans. Not every society practises all three kinds of rite, but
at least one of these forms of initiation is present in every
culture, either in an avowedly religious context, or in a secu-
larised one. Even where the public practice of such rituals
has been discontinued, their presence makes itself felt in folk-
tales and in conscious works of literary art.[7] Eliade's claim is
no less than this: that such rituals, whether they are consciously
performed as religious ceremonies or disguised under other
forms of social interaction, constitute the basic expression of

man's religious awareness. *Rites de passage*, initiatory rituals of all kinds, are socially significant because they are universally prevalent. They are socially necessary because they bind people and communities together. Above all, they are vital to the study of religion, and to our understanding of man's religious consciousness, because they validate the worth of that study. They provide irrefutable evidence as to the existence of that consciousness as a primary human experience.

The instinct which finds expression in corporate rituals, which chooses rituals as its proper way of expressing itself, is the instinct of society, the movement on the part of individuals to establish social identity and social belonging. It is man's need to demonstrate and present himself in relation; to demonstrate this fact about himself, that he lives in relation; to present himself as himself, in a meaningful and explicit action; to reassure himself in the demonstration of inter-dependence and co-inherence; to define his own limits and the limits of his world; to establish a present state of being and to point to a future. *To establish a present, while pointing to a future*; here the instinct becomes specifically religious. In the initiatory scenario, the typical rite, man shows himself to be the grain that will grow through its own dying. He suffers and dies in symbol in order to live in a new way. He returns in order to start out afresh. At this basic level, rites are about life itself. They fall naturally into the shape of the initiatory scenario because they embody reality, rather than some intellectual construct or contrived truth. 'Religious man' knows that to achieve his destiny he must continually start again, which means, in effect, that he must continually die to the past and be re-born into the future.[1] Really to transcend himself, really to reach out towards otherness, he must acknowledge the essential inadequacy of his present state in a salutory gesture of release, a movement of the soul which is both harsh and final. Thus the present is surrendered, and the future secured. A man may know this primal truth in any one of very many ways, in the sense he may make use of different languages, different theologies or mythologies, to express it to himself. But so long as he is aware at all of his religious identity, he is never unaware of this fundamental aspect of that identity.

Certainly, science would make nonsense of all such ideas. Science remains itself, moving in the linear fashion which especially characterises it and marks it as being 'scientific' – suffering setbacks, making mistakes, but always going onwards of its own volition and according to its own laws, confident of its ability to assess present experience in the light of the past. But science has no way of knowing what religion knows immediately and without being told; that the present still stands under judgement at the hands of the future – and that the price demanded is always a death. This is the principle datum of religious knowing; and its primary form is not the sermon, but the rite.

2 The Defence of Ritual

Religion's primary form is the rite, the basic initiatory scenario; and the autonomy of religion, its separate and unique identity, is revealed in the rite's universal prevalence, and in its consistency from culture to culture. All the same, it must be admitted that this is not an idea which is likely to commend itself without misgiving to many Christian people. As we said to begin with, most of us tend to have mixed feelings about rituals. It is possible, some might say, to be *too* basic. Christian people are particularly likely to say this; and they would go on to say that Christianity differs from other religions because of its genuine historicity. Christianity is concerned with doctrines and beliefs about a historical person, and not with modes of organising and expressing man's primitive religious awareness. Christianity's uniqueness does in fact lie in its historical nature. It is not the same as other religions. Jesus is not a 'mythical hero'. All this is quite true – for Christians it is vitally true. However, the fact remains that there are similarities among *all* religions, similarities which allow us to call them religions, and which concern the religious consciousness in general. These similarities are important because the religious consciousness itself is important. It is the raw material for our beliefs, the wood for our Cross. It is not my intention to suggest that all rites are equally significant for Christians; but only to point out that ritual itself is valuable and worth defending, even for those who have 'put on the fulness of Christ'. Christians agree that their sacraments are important channels of God's grace; our intention here is to draw attention to a neglected – even a despised – dimension of their importance.

In this chapter we shall try to answer some of the main criticisms which have been levelled against religious ritual. First of all, and mainly with regard to this chapter, I ought perhaps to explain what I mean by 'the rite'. It has been customary, and is still considered correct, to make a distinction in Christian ecclesiastical writing between 'rites' and 'ceremonies' – 'a rite is a form of service, while ceremony is the method of its performance'. However, I have been using the word rite to mean both things at once, and I intend to go on using it in this way. This is not out of any intention to be perverse, nor is it because I am unwilling to admit that a distinction can, and in some cases ought to be, made between notation and execution in an act of corporate worship. Most of the time, however, it is a distinction that I purposely want to avoid. Most of the time I am talking about ritual as a unity, as a plotted happening, an acted statement. If there is a sense in which a rite is always a ceremony, because it is intended to be treated as one, and only becomes itself when it comes to life in the act of worship, and a ceremony is always a rite, because it is the embodiment of images and ideas which have been consciously formulated and arranged, then this is the sense in which I have been using, and intend to go on using, 'rite' and 'ritual'.

The actual authorship of religious rituals, whether invented or evolved, would seem to be difficult to discover. They represent a codification of religious experiences in the form of images and propositions which are almost certainly extremely ancient. Christian rituals, which tend to be of a literary nature, and certainly stress 'rite' rather than 'ceremony', can be traced back, in inspiration and often even in phraseology, far beyond the liturgiologists to whom they are ascribed. The compilers of more primitive rites – those artists in images whom Levi-Strauss calls 'bricoleurs' – retained material in their finished productions which represents the very first expressions of the religious awareness, when men first looked at the world and themselves and wondered, and turned their wondering into worship. We can no more trace when the rite was originally envisaged than we can discover when it was originally performed. But we may be sure that we only distort the truth when we try to divide the two events, the rite's creation and its performance, in our own minds.

But this is not only true about primitive rites. Liturgy is art; it is drama. To see it as anything else is to destroy its real existence. Good liturgy, like good drama, acts itself out within the imagination. Even the Book of Common Prayer 'acts better than it reads'. The rite is the complete experience, the finished product. As it is celebrated, the rite has certain distinguishing marks. It is serious, because it speaks of holy things. It has the life which belongs to holy things, and it has it in communicable form. This is the holiness of the thing that is entirely other, the life of the thing that is fully shared. Thus the rite is always intensely self-conscious, even at its most spontaneous. It possesses a unique quality of differentness from other experience. It builds a shell around itself in order to preserve this conscious experience of doing holy things – and woe betide anyone who, however inadvertently, breaks that shell, the baby who presumes to cry in church, or the sightseer who didn't realise that there was a service in progress. It can be serious even when it is being hilarious, as in the traditional entertainments which accompany Irish wakes for the dead, when penalties are imposed on those who refuse to take part, or in the time-honoured ceremonies of 'crossing the line' at sea. Always, in all its various manifestations, from the comparatively trivial to the momentous and awe-inspiring, the rite takes itself with the utmost seriousness and commands our respect. And it is always easier to criticise the rite from the outside than the inside. Once the observer becomes the participant he finds that his rational objections have become subtly less forceful than they used to be.

A. *Christian Objections to Religious Ritual*

1. Christianity regards Gods as different from man not merely quantitatively but qualitatively. God is not merely 'man writ large'. He is entirely other than man. This is 'the common ground upon which the Hebraic religions all stand'.[1] Indeed, it is because God is infinitely 'above' the world that His 'coming down into' the world is wonderful. There has never been any confusion about this. However, we may trace a movement in twentieth-century theology towards repudiating 'liberal' tendencies to regard God as immanent in the world in a way which comes near to an actual identification of the divine with the human spirit. This movement is not confined to Protestant writers — indeed, the Roman Catholic theologian von Hugel powerfully asserts the unconditioned transcendence of divinity — but it is in the work of Rudolph Otto and Karl Barth that it finds its most notable expression. Otto draws attention to the feeling of awe which men experience in the presence of the 'mysterium tremendum'; it was he who made current the description of God as 'the altogether Other'. Barth develops the proposition that, with regard to the ideas and experiences of men, the action of God cannot avoid being something totally strange and paradoxical, in Barth's term something 'impossible'. Barth describes the suggestion that there is any direct way, any non-paradoxical connection, between human culture, and the 'impossible possibility' of God as 'sentimental, liberal, self-deception'.[2]

Indeed, it would be possible to claim that what Kierkegaard referred to as the 'infinite qualitative difference' between man and God, time and eternity, lies at the heart of any theological position which is distinctively Protestant — in other words, which preserves the original insights of Luther's archetypal experience of 'salvation through despair'. It is only on the under-

standing that God is unreachable that He is reached; and so
Karl Heim paints a picture of God who works upon the life of
this world from a wholly different dimension,[3] and Rudolf
Bultmann[4] aims at setting aside all 'mythological' formula-
tions concerning the action of God within the human environment as 'scientific' and not 'faithful' – that is, as so many
attempts to give an inauthentic reasonableness to the totally
unreasonable response of faith. The Christ of faith, says Bultmann, is the unknown Christ of the present moment, He who is
not yet known and understood, and not the Christ of history
and myth, the Christ of knowledge. Knowledge, understanding,
the revelation of perfect order, belong to the sphere of Divinity;
men, on the other hand, live by grace alone, by what is vouchsafed to them of that order, that completeness and perfection –
that holiness. The human sphere, say these writers, is always the
world of contingency, of a spoiled freedom, where nothing is
whole, nothing finished and complete. Our religions belong to
this sphere – even our 'Christian religion', seen as a way of
thinking, writing, or speaking about God. Truth in religion,
then, is understood by these writers as, humanly speaking, a
negative thing, *subsisting in the difference between* God and our
various religious ideas and systems – in the primal religious
demand which precedes all cultural expressions to the extent of
negating them. Man's religious truth is to be located in his
hunger for the Divine; simply in his hunger. And it is a hunger
no ritual actions can possibly satisfy – indeed it is a kind of
blasphemy to suppose that they could.

2. Such, then, is the theological objection to ritual. How are we
to answer it? First, by pointing out that it is in this experience
of a total separation from the essential being of God, and the
irresistible pull which the separation exerts, that religious ritual
actually originates. *Because* God is so very far away from His
world, the religious instinct of men moves them in an attempt
to bring the world to Him, to offer it up to Him. They do not
think that the world is worthy, in the sense of being sufficiently

holy or perfect, to be presented to God; but neither are they themselves worthy. They see themselves as part of the world, part of the *mise en scène*. If they come, their world must come too. Thus they do not come *out* of the world. The impossibility of God, and the attraction that impossibility exerts, is acknowledged as a part of their reality, a part of their environment. They do not repudiate their own reality, in acknowledging a superior one. Evelyn Underhill describes this instinct for worship as it exists before it has been sophisticated by any ideas about the superior perfection of mind, or intellect, over matter, as a movement from God to man which begins at the God-ward end, in the impenetrability of Divine mystery, and 'broadens out' at the man-ward end to include and sanctify all that is human. It is the religion itself, the impossible relationship of man with God, which links culture and Divinity, and makes religious behaviour, religious rituals and theologies, in all their 'pathetic childishness', meaningful and worthwhile. We have already said that the rite is the expression of the primal religious relation, the *language* of that relation; this view is shared by Evelyn Underhill.[1]

The purpose of religious ritual, then, is to proclaim the authenticity of *human* reality – the finite world of men and women. Thus ritual externalises those ideas and theories about the meaning of reality which are given doctrinal form in the dogmas of the creation and preservation of men and their responsibility to God. It makes a statement about God in human terms. 'Finite realities' are used for the conveyance of 'infinite truth'. The intention is straightforward and honest. Ritual proclaims the difference between God and man, and at the same time sanctifies the things of men by exhibiting them in the same context as divine things. Thus, the great danger which

---

[1] 'Here we obtain a clue to the real significance of these rituals and ceremonies common to almost every creed, which express the deep human conviction that none of the serial events and experiences of human life are rightly met, unless brought into relation with the Transcendent; that all have more than a natural meaning and must be sanctified by reference to the unseen Powers.' Evelyn Underhill, *Worship*, p. 21.[5]

ritual avoids is the danger of the confusion of man and God. Lifted up to God, man appears as blessedly himself; in a series of ritual actions which express and demonstrate his self-understanding, his aspirations, powers, and limitations, man shows himself as, before God, he really is.

Such an undertaking requires courage. Men do not readily allow themselves to appear in the context of divinity; especially in the context of the towering transcendence of the God of Christian theology. It also requires an honest humility. This is seen in the willingness of men to accept the fact of their own finitude, a finitude which is total and ultimate – as ultimate as the transcendence of the God they are bold to encounter. The biblical revelation of his acceptability to the Father, the 'impossible' worthiness which is his through life and death of the Son, and the biblical invitation to a meeting with both Father and Son which requires the performance of meaningful actions and not simply the recollection of ideas and the thinking of thoughts, urges the Christian towards the sacramental encounter and towards ritual.

Second, as ritual belongs to the humanity of men, so that they cannot avoid it if they are to worship, so it pertains to the humanity of Christ. If the movement of men towards God is in fact natural to mankind, if it is a natural instinct of worship, a native sacrality, however imperfect, then it must constitute a part of that humanness which was perfected by the Incarnation. It must be at least potentially good; it must always be held to have a value of its own; and the notion of its value must be preserved. Louis Bouyer,[6] in *Rite and Man*, distinguishes two movements in Christian thought, which detract from a recognition of the true worth of this natural God-ward movement. On the one hand there is the tendency to stress the human aspects of Christianity 'in such a way that its individuality, along with its divinity, is in danger of disappearing'. The sacraments appear as the evidence of the complete sanctification or sacralisation, in Christ, of all human things in a totally new way – that is, according to an entirely new notion of the sacred, by which the 'natural' division between sacred and profane has ceased to be of any account.[2] Man himself, rather than man as he turns to God, is naturally sacred, and his worship is simply the expression of his divinity. On the other hand, says Bouyer, the sacraments may be regarded as 'pure products of authority', owing nothing of their significance to any human element whatever. Both attitudes (Bouyer distinguishes them as the Nestorian and Monophysite heresies) are equally misguided; for the action of Divinity is to redeem and restore human truth rather than to replace it: 'The Incarnation does not lead to the disappearance of natural sacredness, but to its metamorphosis.' Man is not swallowed up by God in Christ, but met and transformed through Him.

3. The Christian objection to ritual is met more often in its ethical or behavioural form than in its purely theological one, however. Throughout the ages, Christians have been haunted by a dread of turning the means of grace into an occasion of sin. What happens when inner intention falls beneath outward behaviour? May not the sacramental action, even if it is theologically legitimate, mask an inner emptiness on the part of the worshipper? May not the gap which occurs so often in a man's experience, between what his heart knows and his actions reveal, occur in his religious life also? And if this is so, will not his religious life be a mere pretence, an outward crust of formal 'holiness' hiding an interior apathy, or even rebellion?

Protestantism in particular has been preoccupied with such questions ever since Martin Luther. 'In wave upon wave the Reformation has continued to thunder against the empty encrustation of ritual.'[6] The danger is not simply that rites tend almost inevitably to 'lose heart' and become overformal, but also that, in their emptiness, they lend themselves to a more positive evil, that of idolatry. Without the total involvement of a worshipping heart and mind, ritual can easily degenerate into magic, a series of techniques to control reality. It is because

[2] This is the view of such contemporary Protestant writers as Harvey Cox.

of this positive fear of magic and idolatry, of the religion of the unenlightened and unregenerate, that the primacy of grace, the precedence of God's action over man's response, is sometimes asserted in such a way that it can become hard to reconcile with the doctrine of the Word made flesh. In *Rite and Man*, Bouyer has pointed out that the more we endeavour to liberate the Word of God from its fleshly accompaniments, the further we get from receiving it as God's Word for us. Action, the actualisation in space and time of the idea, 'belongs to the original native essence of the word'. When the spoken word takes the place of the forms of corporate ritual, nothing is left but a religious intellectualism – just as, where the word loses its sacred meaning, there is nothing left but 'senseless superstition'. The response of men to Holy Spirit, if it is to be properly human, must be embodied, must have concrete expression. However creaturely, however theocentric, our worship is, it must obey the rules inherent in its creatureliness. We are able to realise nothing, and nothing is fruitful for us, until it has been submitted to our way of being and becomes a part of our world of space and time. Our very desires, convictions, attitudes, and insights depend upon their expression in deeds and words, however inadequate that expression may be; and the stronger the emotion, the more firm the conviction, the more powerful the impulse towards its realisation in significant action.

The indivisibility of human personality, that union of being and doing which is a man or a woman, is mirrored in the indivisible union of word and rite in worship. Ritual weaves speech, gesture, rhythm, and structured ceremonial into a form of worship, which is expressive of man's way of being in the world – that is not as an idea, but as a person; it 'unites his physical, mental and emotional being in a single response to the Unseen',[5] within the specific conditions of humanness. The attempt to respond to God outside the order within which He has placed us, and in which He reveals Himself to us, cannot be spiritually or psychologically successful. Evelyn Underhill talks about the 'garment for God' woven by our imagination. As we have explained, there is not, or should not be, any suggestion that this 'garment' is theologically 'possible' – only that it is anthropologically inevitable. Once this is really understood, the ancient horror of idolatry retreats into the background. Impossible truths, incredible understandings, which reach beyond intelligence and defy logic are wordlessly demonstrated and realised in sacramental ritual. The response which is forced from man by his awareness of divine transcendence does not try to avoid the issue of its own ineptitude. In proclaiming its own humanness it proclaims the impossibility of addressing God in His own language, the unknowable language of the Unconditioned. It is in this proclamation of its own limitation, this showing forth of its own true identity as a human construct involving human actors, that religious ritual is justified. Because the ritual response is so natural to man, it emerges as the purest way of worshipping available to him. In this way, there can be no confusion between God who is Spirit, and his worshippers who draw near to Him in the frankness of their own spirit, according to their own truth. For what is this humanness of worship but the coming together of word and rite in a relation that symbolises not only man's identity as incarnate soul, but also his way of being in the world, which is always the way of relation, the specific existential mode of incarnate beings?

As man presents himself to God as he is, mind and body co-inhering in one human personality, so word and rite co-inhere in human worship. Religious ritual is thus 'the typical human action inasmuch as it is connected with the word as the expression and realisation of man in the world, and to the degree that this expression and realisation are immediately and fundamentally religious'.[6] It was, in Bouyer's phrase, the 'external objectivization' of the word that reduced the rite to a series of techniques; but the counter-attack of intellect is almost equally destructive of true worship. The over-intellectualised word acts directly upon ritual itself, which it regards as a persistently irrational act, the flight from reason into an efficacious symbolism that defies reason – in other words, into magic and idolatry. The various anti-ritualist movements within the Christian Church are only to be understood as reactions to a religion which always runs the risk of degenerating, if not into magic, then at least into superstition, as indeed happened during the Middle Ages – and it was, in the first place, the laudable desire to preserve the simple intelligibility of church services that led the Reformers to prize intellectual clarity above all things and so to lose all idea of meaningful action in worship. 'In the end,' says Bouyer, 'a religion's truth was placed in its intelligibility, which was itself conceived as being something clear and evident.'[6]

Thus, in an atmosphere which distrusted symbolism, there was one symbol which remained, and remains, highly prized. Divine reality in human terms, within the present, is the word of scripture:

'God is nothing but his law and promises; to imagine any other thing of God than that is damnable idolatry'.[3]

The gesture of God, it is implied, is always the word, spoken and written. His symbolic communication is transmitted and received via the faculty of hearing – 'dumb ceremonies are no sacraments but superstitions' concludes Tyndale. The word is communicated verbally, by speaking. In this way it is hoped to avoid the dangers inherent in doing, in acting out the message, which savours on the one hand of technology, the simply mechanical, and on the other of what is worse, idolatry, the introduction of human instrumentality into the sphere of divine Spirit. The sacraments, it is maintained, mediate not the presence of God, but His message to men. Their value consists in their being explained and explicable. 'The word when preached,' says Calvin, 'makes us understand what the visible sign means.'[4]

There is no notion of a meeting of persons, human and

[3] W. Tyndale, *The Obedience of a Christian Man*, Parker Soc., Tyndale, p. 174.
[4] J. Calvin, *The Institutes of Christian Religion*, 4. 14. 14.

Divine, under sacramental forms, which is immediate and un-explained. Symbolism, sui generis, is not to be considered – everywhere, explanation creeps in to destroy the symbol. Protestantism proposes an interior division *within* the sacrament between symbolic form and propositional content, so that, instead of being the unknowable in its own form of knowledge, the Word made flesh for men, the sacrament appears as an explicit message about God out of scripture, the bread and wine being reduced to a mere 'visual aid' to the intelligence of the worshipper.[5] Thus the word, by striving to be nothing more than a word, is actually prevented from becoming one.

Indeed, everywhere in Classical Protestantism we are faced with the idea of an immediate verbal inspiration which is 'evident and clear of itself, forcing, by its own evidence and clearness, the well-disposed to assent, irresistibly moving the same thereunto'.[6] The Quaker objection to formal worship is an extreme example; however it is, in a sense, archetypal, for it illustrates the end towards which all Protestant thought tends.

4. Between this complete rejection of any willed human contribution to worship, and a positive appreciation of the value and significance of ritual forms, lies the main territory of Protestant thinking on the subject. At its most generous the attitude is one of forced acceptance, certainly not of welcome. Because they are human beings, Christians are obliged to express themselves in ways which are open to perversion, and particularly to the temptation to 'manipulate' the world in an attempt to secure God's favour by a technique, thus adopting the disposi-

[5] 'His explanations turn his preaching into a matter-of-fact lesson, and the rites into a simple illustration of this lesson.' L. Bouyer, op. cit., p. 60.

[6] R. Barclay, *The Chief Principles of the Christian Religion as professed by the people called the Quakers.* 'All true and acceptable worship to God,' says Robert Barclay, 'is offered in the inward and immediate moving and drawing of his own spirit, which is neither limited to places, times or persons. All other worship, then, both praises, prayers and preachings, which man sets about in his own will ... whether they be a prescribed form as a liturgy, or prayers conceived extemporarily by the natural strength and faculty of the mind ... they are all but superstitions, will-worship, and abominable idolatry in the sight of God.' – Proposition, XI.

tion of creator instead of that of a creature. Ritual, it is alleged, is notably a 'work'; the bible is called to witness that men should worship God according to faith and not according to works – 'God delighteth not in the noise of the trumpets,' says Tyndale, 'but in the faith of his people.' (*Baptism, Body and Blood of Christ.*)

God is not to be thought of as being susceptible to man's ingenuity. And just as men cannot influence Him in any artificial way, so He, for His part, is not disposed to make use of the works of men as a means of communicating with them. Ritual 'blinds men's pitiable minds in superstition, so that they repose in the appearance of a physical thing rather than in God Himself'.[7]

In other words, ritual belongs to the old dispensation, to the era which has already been superseded by the coming of the potentiality of the kingdom. Christians are exhorted to direct their minds to the future, to the time when 'forms' will no longer be necessary, for the things of this world, which still interpose themselves between men and God, will have no more force or significance, and worship will be 'pure and undefined', free from 'the pomp of ceremonies', which are 'abrogated by (Christ's) coming as Shadows vanish in the clear light of the sun'.[8]

5. It must, I think, be admitted that there is a profound religious truth in that awed sense of 'otherness' and utter transcendence of the spiritual, and the horrified perception of the hopelessness, the profanity, of all attempts to represent it, which underlies this trend to an imageless and unembodied worship. It is felt that the qualitative difference between the two realities, the reality of God and the reality of man, does not, *cannot*, permit the erection in ritual of a 'third reality' in which God and man can meet. Any such erection must be a creation of men, and so,

---

[7] J. Calvin, *Institutes*, 4. 4 and 25.
[8] J. Calvin, op. cit., 4. 4 and 25. For John Wesley's attitude, which is remarkably similar to Calvin's, see 'The Way to the Kingdom', Sermons, p. 74.

in the context of divinity, unavoidably profane. Ritual is artificial; God is not to be imagined as associating Himself with human artifacts in this way. Admittedly, this is not in the first place meant to imply any positive rejection of human things on the part of God, but simply to avoid any suggestion that the initiative in the Divine-human encounter could under any circumstances lie with men. Through the Spirit God gives and men receive – they do not contrive the manner and location of their receiving. Indeed, the manner and the location are not, in the long run, important. They belong to the finitude which awaits sanctification. The theological purpose of the finite is, quite straightforwardly, to direct men towards its opposite, to proclaim a divine presence by means of a human absence. Matter, it seems, *still* needs justifying, and such justification, it is suggested or at least implied, can be found in its paradoxical value, as that which points away from itself.

'The function of the sacrament,' says Calvin, 'is to help the otherwise weak mind of man so that it may rise up to look upon the height of spiritual mysteries.' Religion, the church, the sacraments are valued, then, for what they are *not*, rather than for what they are. They 'do not possess positive content, but must always be understood negatively'.[2] They are valued as expressions of humanness in order to be rejected for precisely the same reason. For Christians, they have no reality of their own – they allow reality to emerge dialectically. And so we see that, within the mechanism of corporate ritual, myth is given precedence over rite, explanation or rationalisation over expressive action, and true human worship is vitiated as surely as if the opposite had happened. Ritual, as such, is dead. The flesh is not so much redeemed and restored as denied and dismissed. Instead of a renewal of relation we have an immolation.

The incarnational truth of Christianity does not seem to shine very brightly here. Calvin urges us to reject all 'carnal' thinking about Christ. As milieu of man's response to God, intellect is much preferred to any other function of human personality. Several writers have drawn attention to a Puritan confusion of the concrete and the finite – implying that that which is not the former is in some way released from being the latter – and to the tendency to confine the notion of idolatry to the products of the image-making faculties of the mind, while assuming that the purely cognitive functions of intellect provide a meeting place with God which escapes the charge of 'impossibility'. Louis Bouyer describes how the determination to stress the transcendence of God at the expense of His immanence can sometimes lead to 'an over-weening rationality' making a 'supreme idol of the intelligence'; Evelyn Underhill comments that an idolatry of abstractions, of the abstracting faculty itself, cannot be much better than an idolatrous attitude towards concrete things.

6. Not much better – and far less easily discerned and remedied! Here we have arrived at the very heart of the matter. For what exactly *is* 'idolatry'? Christians are used to taking the word to mean the denial of a spiritual reality – for them the reality of Holy Spirit – and the attribution of total significance to concrete things. For example, a Christian psychopathology, such as Dr Frank Lake's, would be held to be a truly spiritual venture, diametrically opposed, in its preoccupation with the power of Holy Spirit, to all that is idolatrous. However, any refusal, rejection, or mitigation even, of the *incarnational*, in which flesh and spirit are one in mutuality and wholeness, is a distortion of that very humanity which was assumed by the Godhead in Christ's Incarnation. Personality may be attacked from either side. A parallel idolatry to that of concrete form without spiritual content exists in the exaltation of 'spirit' in its formless state, as if such a thing were possible, within human experience. Dr Lake, in his suspicion of structure in relationships, a suspicion which he shares with a whole generation of 'existentialist' psychopathologists, might be held to resemble the 'demythologising' theologians, whose efforts to distinguish content from form in the New Testament are evidence of a traditional Puri-

tan distrust of structures for belief. Rudolf Bultmann's definition of Christianity as 'authentic existence' belongs to this
tradition, and shares its strength in terms of inducement to
ethical action in the present, at the cost of sharing also its
notable weakness with regard to a certain lack of enthusiasm
for the faith as involved in physical nature, concerned with
bodies and concrete objects as vehicles of spirit.

Worship, to be authentic, must represent the real attitudes
and intentions of the worshipper: so that, in the last resort, all
depends upon the spiritual conviction and sincerity of the individuals taking part in any religious ritual. This is both true
and fundamental. The Reformers were right to point it out.
Indeed, if worship is to be kept alive as a genuine witness to
experience, it must be pointed out again and again. However it
is certainly possible to argue that in focusing so much attention
throughout the ages upon the necessity for one kind of ritual
honesty, men have sometimes fallen prey in their thinking to a
more subtle kind of deception. The body is certainly capable
of lying about the soul; but the soul is also capable of contributing to a lie about itself, its own identity and significance.
To attach *the wrong kind of* significance to the interior dispositions of men is certainly as far removed from true Christian
holiness as to consider a certain disposing of their outward
presence and actions the sole object of God's requirements. On
the one hand we have religion which is automatic and external
– 'a fixed formula, which people recite without feeling or mood
of devotion – untouched both in heart and mind';[9] on the other
we have the attribution of an exaggerated metaphysical significance to man's 'inner life', an unconscious, or semiconscious,
exaltation of the cognitive and affective aspects of religion as
the real locus of divine activity. Thus, the mind, while not
actually divine itself, at least 'speaks the same language' as
divinity. The organ of response, which is the locus of an experienced freedom and acceptance, is allowed to stand for the
whole organism. The divine–human encounter becomes located

[9] E. Heiler, *Prayer*, p. 65, quoted by E. Underhill.[5]

not in the relationship between the world and God, but actually *inside* men, in the relationship between body and mind, by which the latter is held to be agreeable to God and susceptible to divine influences in a way that the former is not. Thought, or mental activity (in other words a distinguishable part of man) is somehow able to 'leap the gap' between man and God in a way which is denied to man's earthly nature. The implication is that, in fact, men have *two natures*, an 'earthly' and a 'spiritual'. The 'spiritual nature' of man is redeemed or divinised (or is susceptible to redemption or divinisation), the 'earthly' nature is not. Which is hardly a Christian idea.

This concentration on mind is a distortion of human experience, which is unavoidably psychosomatic. Men are 'imprisoned within the actual'. Theologically speaking they remain not Spirit, but Flesh. Psychologically, they experience themselves as 'en-fleshed'. The actual physical presence, the bodily self, plays an unavoidable part in those spiritual matters, those questions of value, purpose, or justification which are considered to be the concern of the mind. We do not move where we like; we are largely pushed about by our bodies; and not only in a metaphorical sense. Always, our bodies and minds have both a limiting and an extending effect upon each other. Intentions and circumstances, minds and bodies, interact to produce the specific human mode of being in the world. Information about this is not adequately conveyed by statements, because man is not simply statement, he is action as well. He is an *acted statement* – and his actions and the limitations imposed on them by his bodily presence, and their extension in the production of his mental activity, all affect the nature of his statement. Thus, to be understood, to be seen as himself, in interpersonal terms to *be* himself, man requires *demonstration* rather than exposition. He will be understood in the moment of meeting, when he is met as himself, or in a succession of such moments, or he will not be understood at all. For he is a creatures for whom spatial extension within three dimensions are facts of existential significance affecting all his experiences.

Objectively he is true to himself in movement and interaction. Subjectively he *feels* true to himself in relation.

The process of intellectualisation stems from a fear of encounter with other people as they are; that is, as demonstrably 'other', and it has the effect of suggesting that the meeting with other people, and with God, is 'possible' in a human way – i.e. it rejects the sacramental mode in favour of an implied mental contact with God, which cannot *be seen* to be impossible, as can ritual and sacrament. Protestantism seems always to concentrate on the interior, the private, the existential.[10] It is as though the intention were always to intellectualise immediacy, always to interpose consideration between the persons in the saving encounter, always to comment on the nature and significance of what is happening rather than allowing it simply to happen. Certainly it is true that, in the pure light of reason, the impossible stands forth in all its impossibility, as unapproachable and wholly judgemental; and this is a salutory experience for the conscience. But is a man only his conscience? Is he only the formulated experience of relationship with the Other? It was to the *embodied* conscience, the *conditioned awareness* that the Incarnate Word came – and it is *this* conscience, *this* awareness which is convicted and redeemed. It was surely not in order to introduce this kind of interior division between a responsiveness of 'pure intelligence' and an experience of a recalcitrant 'life of the body' that Holy Spirit was given at Pentecost. For all its assertion of the freedom and autonomy of Holy Spirit, Protestant thinking recoils from the vague and not yet formed world of uncertain possibility which is the real sphere of art and of imagination, because this world ever eludes the grasp of intellect. Kierkegaard[7] tells us that 'Christianity retires from the sensuousness of imagination into

---

[10] 'Protestants,' writes Francis Huxley, 'have always suspected the worst of man's physical body, and have damped down on the images it spontaneously produces in its efforts to give life a shape; language and verbal experiences are made to define the centre of activity of the ontological self, while visual images and non-verbal perceptions are stripped of their power.' Francis Huxley, *Contact*, January, 1967. Huxley goes on to refer to the demythologising theologians as 'the great schizoids of our time'.

intellectual inwardness'. The divine image is seen here as pure intellectuality and the victory of Spirit as the defeat of everything that is formless or irrational, or receives its form from men and not from God.

Perhaps we can find a clue to all this in that experience of conversion which is the definitive experience of Protestant Christianity. Protestantism focuses attention upon the subjective and the existential; that is, upon the personal faith–experience. Not only is this intensely interior and private, but it also involves a powerful awareness of dialectic and polarity, of opposing forces and conflicting ideas.[11] The convert feels that what is happening to him concerns his whole personality, but its focus is the very centre of his personal being, his as it were 'organ of relation'. This part of him, he feels quite positively, almost tangibly, to be changed and renewed. It now belongs to God in an entirely new way. We might say that the Protestant becomes the Puritan when this experience of a renewed mind and heart presents itself as so fixed, so reified, so much a concept, as to constitute all significant reality for him – as an idea, that is rather than as a happening; when this new relation, which is so powerfully existential that it excludes the possibility of any other essential relation, becomes permanently fixed in the terms of the original experience, so that it can no longer move freely, but must for ever retain its former shape. Thus, that individualistic stress which is the life of Reformed theology both reinforces, and is itself reinforced by, the tendency in the direction of a Manichaean rejection of all which resists mind. For although it is the whole man who, as a result of the conversion-event finds himself in a new relation to God, it is his intelligence, his faculty of abstraction, which draws conclusions about this relation. The violent nature of the experience, its identity as 'krisis', contributes to its implacable concreteness as a *concept* – 'this is what happened, this and nothing else!'

[11] Vde for example, Tillich's[8] description of faith as 'accepting acceptance because one is unacceptable'. (*The Courage To Be.*)

7. It follows from this, that the faculties of imagination and intuition, the experience and enjoyment of the sensuous, may come to be rejected because they seem to avoid the central *theological* issue, which concerns the mind. It is the mind, in the sense of the intellect, which is the agent of choice and action, and which is concerned with the serious business of keeping God's commandments – whereas our other faculties are always to some extent engaged in enjoying themselves, producing their own non-rational answers to these ultimate questions about the nature of man and God which the Puritan may no longer even consider asking; behaving, as Kierkegaard says, 'as if life were an opera'. The implication behind Kierkegaard's judgement is that art and life ought not to be considered together, if life is understood as the transformed reality of Christian experience. Life possesses a seriousness, an authenticity, that art can never possess. Art belongs under the heading of man's attempts to achieve a perfection of his own, a paradise of human ingenuity – and thus to avoid the explicit demand of God for perfect sonship, perfect obedience, perfect surrender to grace and subjection to divine reality. All intellectual model-making, all theologising must to the Christian constitute a snare and a distraction, simply because it is 'aesthetic' rather than 'existential'. The terms are Kierkegaard's – but the rejection of the artistic as a suitable expression of the relationship between God and man is considerably older, going back at least as far as Plato.[12]

However, it must be repeated that the identification of religion 'pure and undefiled' with an attitude of mind rather than a disposition of the whole personality in which all the various functions, including the image-making function, are summoned into the divine presence, is not only to be found among Protestants. Indeed Louis Bouyer has said that 'all modern Catholics can be regarded as being unwilling Protestants in this regard'. Nor is it found in all Protestants; indeed, the attitude of

[12] I myself have found it in Calvin's *Institutes* and also in Tyndale. Doubtless it occurs in the writings of other Reformers.

Luther himself to religious ritual stands over against the 'spiritualising' attempts of later writers. We should always remember, says Luther, that Christians are 'bound by the needs of their bodily life'; and this must be acknowledged in their approach to the Divine. But this is still some way from recognising a positive virtue in Christian ceremonial, or expounding a Christian theology of ritual.

8. In all that we have said so far, the main point we have been trying to make is this: that non-ritualistic worship simply is not worship at all, as Christian people understand the term, because it is not honest, honest about men themselves, or about God as He reveals Himself to men. The New Testament tells us that, because of our initiation into Christ, which involves specific and deliberate ritual actions of a corporate nature, we may use the language of homology with God, approaching with boldness to the throne of grace; we may believe and trust that we are his re-adopted children, partakers of his Divinity.[13] But this happens to our whole being, our whole embodied self; our whole person may now use that language,[14] and we may only use it as whole people, not as disembodied intellects, or unthinking automatons. In and through Christ we acknowledge a new wholeness. Something transforming has happened to us.[15] How can we show our understanding in a way which really expresses the nature of that understanding if we shun those rites of response which religion provides us with, the natural and spontaneous dialogue with Divinity allowed by the universal scenarios of religion? How can we find the words to speak to God as a renewed and transformed community if we will not use the proper language?

[13] Hebrews 4: 16; also Ephesians 3: 12; Romans 8: 15; Galatians 4: 5.
[14] I Corinthians 6: 19; Colossians 2: 9, 10; I Thessalonians 5: 23.
[15] II Corinthians 5: 7; Galatians 6: 15; Ephesians 4: 24; Revelation 21: 5 (also Matthew 26: 28; Mark 14: 24; Luke 22: 20, and I Corinthians 11: 25), c.f. Eichrodt, *Theology of the Old Testament*: 'The Mosaic religion ... is not controlled by some concept of duty which is the product of logical construction but by the living reality of God, with all its contradictions.' (p. 111.)

Within Christianity itself, the reality of the 'impossible possibility', the Word become flesh, shines forth in ceremonial acts which do not argue, but simply proclaim, and by their refusal to defend themselves in argument, stress the ultimate worthlessness of human 'theologising' according to Christian revelation. Surely this is more radical than Barth, more Puritan than Calvin! 'No man hath seen God at any time.'

'The representative pattern, the suggestive symbol, the imaginative projection; all these must be called into play and their limitations humbly accepted if the conditioned creature is to enter into communion with the Holy and so develop his capacity for adoring love,' for, says Evelyn Underhill, 'only insofar as man's worship is firmly rooted in the here and now of our common experience and accepts the conditions imposed by that experience, will it retain its creaturely quality.' But is it necessary to make excuses for the fumbling nature of men's attempts to express the inexpressible? It is in their crudity and inadequacy that their value, their holiness, lies. Frankly and joyfully the cultus proclaims its own limitation. The danger of ritual, its 'idolatry', is located precisely at the point of its failure to do this – where devotion is private and interior, where the mechanics of man's approach to Transcendence are hidden from common view. The perfection of worship, its divine acknowledgement and ratification, lies within a dimension which is beyond any human faculty, emotional intellectual or artistic – the dimension of faith, which precedes any kind of human knowing. In Christian sacramental ritual, man shows himself in his entirety as a creature who is body as well as mind, and whose body and mind are inextricably involved with the conditions of his environment; it is *this* creature who responds to the call of Spirit and who presents himself before the Wholly Other. Having thus established his own intransigent concreteness, his total non-divinity, he has no other means at his disposal, no other credentials to present, than faith. In the language of the basic religious rate he has no direction in which to move but upwards.

9. In ritual, then, a Christian acts out before God his own finitude and the finitude of his constructs and operations, in the faith that even they can lead him to the God who begins where they end. This is the real nature of that 'theatricality' so deplored by the attackers of religious ritual. When man enters the world of worship he enters a world which has many of the characteristics of an artistic creation, a world where 'on every level, phantasy is bound to play a creative and expressive – nay an indispensable – part'.[5] Ritual gives artistic form to corporate experience. And if the experience is to be authentically Christian, it must be corporate, it must find its expression in some kind of social belonging. What von Hugel calls 'the principle of the community' in the cultus is expressed and allowed by the element of artistic contrivance, the conscious effort to provide an expressive framework for a shared understanding about reality. In art and in art alone is the whole man made present – for here alone is thought rendered experiential by involvement and experience rationalised by distance. The thoughts and experiences to be expressed and understood, to be *lived*, in religion are inescapably social, inescapably turned and directed outward towards otherness. And so it is inevitable that the form of art chosen will be the drama.

The proper language for responding to Divinity is the social language of the rite. In every human society which has reached even a rudimentary religious consciousness, worship is given its concrete expression in institutions and ritual acts, which become in their turn, powerful instruments for the stimulation, teaching, and maintenance of the worshipping impulse. The impulse is a social one and it is socially expressed, for basically religion and society are closely associated. This is the relation which is symbolised in liturgy, and which liturgy both expresses and makes actual; for, just as every liturgy has its own self understanding and gives life to its own world-view, so it may be said to preach its own gospel. In ritual, the community learns about itself; that corporate understanding about life and the world which expresses itself artistically in ritual acts and ceremonies, is itself an understanding of life and the world *as corporate*, as a shared reality, in which personal experience is inextricably involved in, and dependent upon, community. The social nature of religious awareness demands its own kind of symbol, which will express and establish the reality of inter-action and inter-dependence, of *relation*. The chosen symbol which lies at the heart of religion, is ritual, and the nature of its working is essentially artistic, in that it is a meeting of content and form, what Mary Douglas calls 'a crystallising of experience'.[9] Thus, through the medium of art, religious feeling is able to reinforce social awareness, a sense of corporate identity, and consequently social action in the world. For a Christian, as John Robinson[10] points out, the sacramental liturgy is recognisably and explicitly a piece of social action. Liturgy, says Dr Robinson, *means* social action, 'the work of the people of God' – and the element of contrivance, the part played by human wills, is justified and redeemed for Christian people because it is ratified by the dominical command.

The symbolism of the sacramental species of the gift of Christ's body and blood is mirrored in the circle of communicants, mirrored and diffused. As the first symbolises Christ's glorified natural Body, so the second symbolises his Mystical Body, in which the corporateness is sacred and the sacredness corporate. 'The content of the sacrament', says Adrienne von Speyr[11] 'is love which is always an indivisible unity of love of God and for one's neighbour'. Thus all mankind in its social action and social belonging is signified in the real presence of the group of Christians who kneel or stand before the altar. The very grouping of those who receive, their actual spatial disposition within the sanctuary, fortuitous and haphazard as it is, is nonetheless full of meaning, and attains a symbolic purity of outline, the completeness and unity that belong to the symbol alone – simply because it is the group of individuals who communicate with wholeness, and so become whole themselves, whole as a group, to be a sign and source of wholeness within the world.

10. To *conclude* then, ritual may be regarded as 'demonstrated theology' from two points of view. It may be held to *exalt* a God who stands over against the humanness of men; or to *embody* a God who communicates via, or expresses himself in, society. In the sacramental ritual of the people of God, the distance between God and his world is bridged by the sanctification of matter. For these people, in this action, the finite world is made the perfect medium of God. Thus, ritual may be seen to illuminate not only the transcendence of Almighty God, but also, in the light of divine revelation, His immanence in the world of men and things which he creates and sustains. Because of the nature of men and of things, theology, man's understanding of God, demands actual demonstration; because of the nature of God as He reveals himself to the religious consciousness of men, this demonstration must express the truth of divine immanence and transcendence as a miraculous experience of the relationship of otherness.

B.   *The Psychopathological Critique*

We have seen that the tendency of Christian theology has been first to misunderstand, and then, as a result, to distort, the language of ritual. The mistake made by psychopathology and also, traditionally by anthropology, has been to deny its nature as language altogether. The suggestion which was made in Chapter 1, that ritual is an autonomous and self consistent code of communication transmitting ideas 'contained within itself' – that is, ideas which cannot really be expressed in any other way – is not likely to commend itself to the reductionist ideologies of disciplines which cling to scientific methodology.

1. Freud regards ritualistic religion as a kind of group equivalent of obsessional neurosis. Obsessional neurosis is to be regarded, he says, as 'a pathological counterpart to the formation of a religion'.[12] This is why obsessive acts are described as 'ceremonial' behaviour. Indeed, neuroses may be considered to

be private religions in that they involve the 'fundamental re-
nunciation of the satisfaction of inherent instincts', which
in neurosis are sexual, but in religion are concerned with the
autonomy of the ego. Acceptance of this corporate neurosis,
claims Freud, 'spares religious people the task of constructing
a personal one'.[13] According to him, religion is grounded in
fear, and in the need to influence the forces of nature; religious
ritual stems directly from infantile ways of dealing with this
fear. Man, says Freud, does not simply project himself upon
nature by personification; he endeavours to control it by getting into relation with it in accordance with techniques learnt
in early childhood. These techniques invite the same kind of
neurosis as they do in the 'normal' maturation of personality,
which, says Freud, always 'involves a phase of neurosis, sometimes greater, sometimes of less distinctness'. Religions represent and originate from this 'neurotic' phase in the development of humanity as a whole. They are, in fact, a hangover
from the time when mankind was constrained by its own
anxiety to repress the demands of instinct, instead of dealing
with them, 'according to the rational operation of the intellect'.
Thus, religion arose 'like the obsessional neuroses of children,
out of the Oedipus complex, out of the relation to the
father'.[13]

Freud is not saying here that religious people are 'neurotics',
but only that religions originated in 'a neurotic phase of human
development'; in *Totem and Taboo* he puts forward the suggestion that mankind as a whole may have acquired its sense of
guilt, 'the ultimate source of religion and morality ... at the
beginning of its history, in connexion with the Oedipus complex'.[14] It is possible, he says, for an individual to use religion
as an alternative to becoming neurotic, and to find a healing
expression of his private guilt feelings in the practice of religious rituals. The individual, as it were, actually inherits a
neurotic understanding of, or relation to, the world, which he
incorporates within his own psychic structure. If he externalises this understanding and acts in accordance with it, he finds

relief for his own private guilt feelings. The importance of religion is simply this, that it is useful in relieving neurosis, and that it illustrates the proposition that mankind as a whole mirrors the development of the individual. Nothing is lost or gained by talking of the psychological experience of individuals or of groups; the experience is the same. It is always basically an intra-psychic phenomenon; the only reality it refers to is an intra-psychic reality, a mental mechanism of the individual man or woman.

In short, then, religious ritual is a corporate expression of a person's private obsession about himself, his own problems, attitudes, and state of mind, seen in religious terms inherited from 'the childhood of the race'. It is inescapably tied in with the working of Oedipal guilt and gratification, with an ambivalent relation of fear and love towards an ever present father. The figure of the punishing and rewarding father is always present because its image has been remorselessly incorporated in the individual psyche. It is this father-image which bedevils the expression of instinctive desires and emotions, which now have as it were to be slipped past it in disguise, masquerading as the 'symptoms' of obsessional neurosis. The original impulse towards self-gratification is still there 'lurking in the unconscious'[12] (Freud's own phrase), in the form of 'temptation', and 'anxiety' which is the result of temptation. The new state of affairs is never really secure, for the mechanism of repression is constantly threatening to break down; and the ritual behaviour indulged in by the neurotic person – that is the person in whom the libidinal invasion of consciousness with its attendant anxiety is endemic – is a way of compromising between the satisfaction of temptation and the avoidance of anxiety. 'Ceremonial and obsessive acts,' says Freud, 'always reproduce something of the identical pleasure they were designed to prevent.'[16]

[16] 'The psychoanalytic theory of obsessional neurosis is that obsessions are distorted symbolic versions of instinctive desires forbidden by the super-ego (i.e. the punitive father-image) or of the super-ego's prohibitions themselves. The obsessions and compulsions simultaneously allow some substitute gratifi-

2. Beneath the pretence of atoning for the presence in the unconscious of forbidden impulses, neurotic people use formal acts of self-punishment which serve to remind them of the things they have consciously striven to forget. Through the demonstration of expiation and innocence the guilty subject is continually kept in mind. The dialectical force of ritual, its function of *always pointing away* (that is of directing attention away from itself towards what may not otherwise be directly confronted or openly envisaged), which we considered in the previous section, occurs here in a private – an excessively private – form, as the distinguishing mark of psychological malfunction. This structural resemblance between religious rites and private obsessions was overlooked by Freud. As a way of understanding religious behaviour it is considerably more significant than speculation about the content of religious feelings, which must after all always remain speculation and cannot be proved. The essential difference between the two kinds of ritual remains. Religious rites are public and shared. Neurotic ritual is indulged in privately by individuals; even when it is carried out publicly it is mainly concerned with the neurotic person's own psychological economy.

3. Certain 'ego psychologists' repeat the notion that ritual behaviour is an externalisation of repressed feelings. This time, however, the feelings are an expression of personal responsibility, or of conscience, rather simply of the demands of the pleasure principle. Mowrer[15] maintains that we engage in neurotic rituals because we are subject to powerful feelings of guilt. He suggests that neurotic symptoms constitute a means of drawing attention to a moral or ethical mistake on the subject's part, for which the subject is experiencing a very real pain. He quotes Luke 12:14, 'Beware the leaven of the Pharisees; I mean their hypocrisy. There is nothing covered up that

---

cation both of the desire and its prohibition.' M. Argyle, *Religious Behaviour*, 1958.

will not be uncovered, nothing hidden that will not be made known.' Again, the symptoms of neurosis are held to serve the dual function of satisfying the urges which brought the original lapse about and underlining the sufferer's responsibility for it and his feelings of guilt about it. Thus, the rite constitutes a language whose content is its own necessity, its essential and necessary difference from ordinary 'straightforward' communication. This alternative language provides the only way in which the deeply ambiguous experience can be transmitted and expressed – and consequently it affords the only means by which the suffering, guilty person may reveal his condition to the outside world, and so be healed. The direct verbal confession of responsibility proves too painful; but the neurotic code which he employs is his own, designed to fit his unique message; it is how he feels driven to express himself, the only way he can understand himself, the truth about himself. Thus a conscious artifice, a stereotyped and seemingly arbitrary selection of responses, an obvious lie, speaks the plain truth about the subject's guilt and his deep existential need to confess it, once the language of neurosis has been learnt. And it is the subject's intention that we should learn it, indeed we *must* learn it, for only thus may we relieve his intolerable anxiety, the anxiety of an enforced *privacy*, a private hell of loneliness and despair.

4. According to Freud, then, neurotic ritual is amoral, the symptom of a sickness, an 'obsessional neurosis'. People who indulge in it form 'a definite clinical group'.[12] According to later writers, however, it is a lie, a private subterfuge aimed at avoiding the pain which, it is believed, would follow from self-disclosure. Laing,[16] Mowrer,[15] Jourard,[17] Maslow,[18] have all accused 'orthodox' Freudian psychopathology of having made the 'sickness' worse by its treatment of neurotic people in accordance with a clinical stereotype which denies men and women the opportunity to be themselves, to be individuals, to be unique. Freudian psychology, they maintain,

is guilty of depersonalisation in two principle ways, through its theory and through its practice. The theory of orthodox Freudianism ascribes no real authority to the ego as an instrument of choice, and lends itself to a view of the self as almost wholly determined by psychic forces over which it has little or no control, the 'libido', and the 'super-ego', the forces of lust and of fear. Man is trapped between what he *wants* to do and what he *ought* to do, and cannot really *choose* to do anything at all. The practice of Freudianism, on the other hand, is simply the application of this philosophy of psychological determinism; but it is both limiting and dangerous, say the 'ego-psychologists', to apply any systematic philosophy at all in our approach to our fellow human beings, because this encourages a tendency to reduce patients to the condition of clinical stereotypes.

5. For Mowrer, neurosis is the result of unadmitted guilt on the part of the subject. Its symptoms constitute a direct message to that effect. They are 'a lie to cover a mistake'. For other writers, (Maslow[18], Jourard[17], May[19], and Laing[16] and, writing from an avowedly Christian view-point, Drs Paul Tournier[20] and Frank Lake[21]) however, it is not so much an explicit guilt, a clear responsibility for committing certain specific and recognisable sins, which leads to ritual behaviour undertaken for the dual purposes of self-concealment and self-advertisement, but something rather more profound and much harder to isolate and to cure. It is a diffused and generalised frailness of being, which is less likely to be the result of a moral lapse or series of lapses than of an entirely unspecific feeling of inadequacy. Certainly this inadequacy presents itself as guilt, as moral failure; but, say such writers, the inadequacy is better understood as a failure of nerve at the deepest level of a person's being, an 'ontological insecurity'. A neurotic person may be as incapable of committing a real sin as he is of performing an act of real self-sacrifice; indeed, such insecure people find it hard to make a stand, either for good or evil.

If Dr Mowrer reminds us of Frank Buchman, Maslow,[18]

Jourard,[17] and Laing[16] derive from Paul Tillich.[8] However, there is agreement on the main point; that ritual behaviour is the expression of an inner malaise, a codification of feelings that appear to be dangerous to the subject to be expressed openly, but which must nevertheless be expressed; of 'an exquisite vulnerability which learns to cry when amused and smile when sad'.[16] Something must be communicated, but its public meaning need not be the same as its private significance, so long as contact is made. Indeed, it is likely to be the very opposite.

6. Mowrer attacks Freud for denying a man's responsibility for his own sins by explaining all sin away in terms of libidinal forces which are basically impersonal. In one very important respect, however, he himself resembles Freud, and aligns himself alongside the master against his fellow 'psychologists of the ego' (that is, those psychologists of free choice who attribute significance to the reality-changing powers of the conscious mind). Mowrer locates guilt and responsibility in the very place that Freud denies their existence, that is, inside the individual psyche. Guilt, like those libidinal forces which Freud holds responsible for it, is a private concern. The cure for it is to make it public. But for the school of Maslow and Laing, guilt is always essentially *inter-personal*. It is already public in the sense that it is already shared, already between people rather than inside persons. It originates in a primal breakdown of communication which affects all subsequent relationships, and which destroys the ability to make relationships – a breakdown which involves all mankind, but is exaggerated by certain circumstances and events in an individual person's early life, when identity was least well defined and the self least well defended; events which tended to turn him away from his neighbour and in upon himself. This universal ontological weakness, or primal susceptibility, is not caused by individual sins so much as individual sins are caused, or at least compounded, by it. The cure for it is somehow to enable people to face one another as they really are, as they really feel themselves to be. To encour-

age them in community, in corporate responsibility, in breaking through existential privacy and 'false self systems'[16] towards the other. Basically, the cure lies in a transformation of attitudes towards other people within the community itself. The private code of communication must be understood and acknowledged by those to whom it is addressed. Indeed, there must be an exchange of existential codes. Neurosis must be acknowledged as a corporate phenomenon, universal in its implications, its responsibility shared by all.

In fact, of course, any approach to the healing of personality via a stereotype of explanations and expectations cannot be appropriate when we are concerned with relational disorders or disordered relationships. 'A stereotyped relationship' is a contradiction in terms, for relationship is a response to the other in a way which respects and preserves its otherness. The psychopathology that is stereotyped, that constitutes a reified model of personal interaction is a refusal really to look at another person and a decision to look at oneself; and this, according to R. D. Laing, is precisely what the schizoid 'patient' is himself doing. Laing is well known for his advocating the acceptance of mental illness as a particular kind of existential exploration undertaken by a person for reasons of expansion and survival as a person, rather than as a collection of symptoms of disease; it is an adventure into the unknown rather than a capitulation and a collapse. He points out that, to draw up a model of psychological breakdown always involves the claim to know exactly what breakdown is, and so 'precludes the possibility of understanding a patient's disorganisation as a failure to achieve a specifically personal form of unity'. From thinking that a person is like a thing, like a plan, a scheme, a theory, it is only a small step to thinking of people as things. 'We are left with transactions, but where is the individual? the individual, but where is the other.' Thus the possibility of genuine meeting is precluded from the outset.

Here then we have the other side of the coin with regard to inauthentic role playing on the part of the patient or client in a therapeutic relationship. The urge towards self preservation which leads to what Laing calls 'false self systems' is as much aggressive as defensive; that is, it aims to ensure the security of the self by disarming the other. The 'false self' encounters a 'false other', an other which has been included within the new phantasied situation which is represented within the whole 'false-self' complex of stereotyped action and reaction. If Freudian psychopathology is concerned with private rituals which are the exteriorisation of a neurotic limiting of personal reality on the part of individuals, 'existentialist' ego-psychologists draw attention to the involvement of the therapist himself in exactly the same kind of ritual behaviour. 'The therapist may practice what Buber calls "semblance" or "seeming" as chronically as does the patient' – 'a practice', comments Jourard,[17] 'which is inimical to the growth of self in both parties'.

7. Nowadays, says Laing, 'it is the relation between persons which is central in (psychotherapeutic) practice'. However, the interaction of persons in the healing relationship is still regarded as basically anti-ritual. This would seem to be because of a misunderstanding of the role of the formal in relationship, and also because of the determination to follow Freud in interpreting ritual solely in terms of neurotic symptom formation by individuals. It is maintained that the healing encounter will only take place where there is an absence of any kind of stereotyped behaviour on the part of both patient and therapist. The object is everywhere to avoid the structured situation, the tendency everywhere to regard ritual as the symptom of a malaise. Ritual behaviour and the assumption of predetermined roles are inevitably associated with the intention to deceive, or to conceal the truth of a situation, or to avoid the issue of an encounter. The naked ego, we are assured, needs embodiment. If it cannot 'clothe itself in relationship' it will evolve its own structures for defence and aggression, for coping with the needs of survival. Relationship depends on mutual acceptance and

candour. We must acknowledge the facts as they are, rather than as we would like them to be. But it also depends on the existence of recognisable facts, of certain fixed points in a shifting situation. The dependable and recognisable land-marks constitute real presences, allowing the situation to be a situation, so that relationship may take place. Otherwise we have only an idea, and not really even that, for ideas involve and require structure. We have only an aspiration.

We can agree, then, with the psychologists of the ego when, in accordance with Freud's original determination, they insist upon candour in relationships to 'bring to light the hidden things of darkness'; we would certainly differ from their implied assertion that only the unstructured can be candid. The human personality is itself a structure – and it is capable of candour. As it lives in relation to other personalities it is *a structure for candour*, the embodied spirit of frank and honest encounter. Similarly, it makes use of other structures, which it proclaims openly as structures, not attempting to disguise their artificiality. Role-playing can be candid. Candour about structure and role, honesty about the value of contrived circumstances, belongs to an understanding of human existence in the world as it is, the world as sphere of presences which may be brought into relationship with one another.

Ego-psychologists stress the central importance, for health of personality, of mutuality, of meeting and sharing – of communication. They regard the ritualised behaviour of neurotic people as a failed attempt to achieve communication. Neurotic ritual is an alternative language, which does not fulfil its purpose as a language because of a perverse obscurity and paradoxicality; that is, it is contrived both for clarification and obfuscation. But this is because the intention of a neurotic person is simply this, to communicate without real candour, to encounter without relationship. He sends his messages through a carefully constructed 'baffle', an interference network of contradictory signals. In the process, the message becomes 'scrambled' and real communication fails, as indeed it must fail.

There is not enough strength in the genuine signal, not enough basic courage to face the encounter with reality. The messages transmitted by a neurotic person fail to achieve mutuality, fail to elicit the proper response from other people, because he lacks the essential, ontological courage to speak a language which others will recognise and understand. Thus, neurotic symptoms represent a private language, employed through terror of the common relational tongue. In order for a meeting to take place, this language, say the psychologists, must first of all be translated. It is possible, by means of an open gesture of self-giving on the therapist's part to reach the alienated person through his defensive screen of neurotic ritual, and so to help him. The ritual is to be penetrated, either analytically, or, preferably, by exerting the stronger power of personal gift; and the person hiding behind is to be contacted.

Here again we have an unwillingness to consider ritual as valuable in itself. Psychologists try to break the code by explaining it or by passing it by altogether in an effort to remove the barrier from behind by an indirect approach – anything rather than receiving it at its face value. 'But,' they protest, 'its face value is worthless. You can't expect us to waste time on it! It is the person behind the code that counts; the code itself is nonsense.' But the two are not to be separated. In a very real sense, the person *is* the code. The code is the person's existential organisation, his way of being in the world. He is talking nonsense – but he is doing it sensibly, or he is behaving sensibly in doing it. After all, 'nonsense' is all he can talk; it is his message to the world of sense. 'Nonsense' is what he feels himself to be; it is he himself, in his encounter with other people. Neurotic people make their messages obscure on purpose, not only to defend themselves, but with the more positive aim of transmitting an urgent message, a message about obscurity. Ritual speaks for itself and cannot be misinterpreted. It is itself the language of immediate, non-thetic, instant relationship, the code of primal awareness. Words are abandoned as argument, in favour of the unequivocal gesture. The content of the message demands demonstration, not rationalisation; indeed, it must demonstrate itself. 'I speak obscurely because I am obscure – and this is how I am obscure', says the neurotic person. It is not an argument but a cry, a desperate signal. The rite is his sole way of communicating his anguish, for he is unable to get far enough away from his pain, from himself, to achieve any other kind of clarity. He cannot gain the necessary distance from what is happening to give us a rational commentary on his existential situation.

Neurotic people, then, transmit obscure or displaced messages, in order to transmit the message that this is the only kind of message they can transmit, and therefore it is reliable and authentic. We notice once again the paradoxical nature of the rite which neurotic ritual shares with religion, the rite which says 'I am sending a message that cannot be sent, making a gesture that cannot be made, the message and the gesture of my own radical unworthiness, the sign of my negativity.' Certainly the message cannot be sent, nor the gesture made, in any other way. But once we have received this meaninglessness, this piece of nonsense, sent out into the void, as it is, as a piece of information addressed to the other, addressed to *us*, rather than as a symptom to be noted and filed away, then we can reply to it. The only adequate reply, however, is the reply in kind. We cannot acknowledge this signal in our familiar language or argument, for our correspondent has demonstrated that such messages are unintelligible to him in his present state of being by the form of his own message. If we are to reach him we must do so *ritually*.

This then is the state of affairs. We must talk to and with the neurotic person about matters upon which his whole being depends, matters which have become so painful, so stressfully urgent, that he can find no words to show his panic and confusion, but only gestures; and so we too must use the language of ritual. In the shared rite we are able to meet him. Here, and here alone, we are in a position to 'exchange burdens and so fulfil the law of Christ'. Freud confesses himself to be at a loss to explain why rituals resemble the obsessional behaviour of neurotic people, while religion itself has the effect of safe-guarding its adherents from neurosis. Here we have one answer at least: it is because religious rituals are corporate rituals. They do not 'resemble' neurotic rituals, but are the completion of and answer to such rituals. But Freud, of course, could not be expected to know this; he most certainly did not 'speak the right language'!

To return to psychology itself, R. D. Laing and others have written at length about the psychological dependence of the individual self on the achievement of a relationship with other selves. It is only in relation to others that we are ourselves; and the tendencies in the maturing child which promote psycho-logical health are those which are stimulated and developed by the experience of differentiation and relation. If these ten-dencies are consistently thwarted, then psychosis ensues; if they are not adequately provided for, the self retires into itself, and becomes less and less able to reach out for the experience of otherness, of contact-in-separation, by which it lives. We note that this experience of the relation of beings who are separate and distinct, of an alternating sameness and difference, is at its most powerful in corporate ritual. Here the sense of aloneness and vulnerability which dogs the individual is pub-licly and unanimously expressed in a crowd. Here, the experi-ence of the self is ratified by the testimony of others. It ceases to be a painful experience when it is shared, for it becomes a feeling about the whole social unit. The self is reinforced in its own identity, its own self-hood, by contact with what is quite distinctly and discernibly not itself, yet comes together with it in an experience of mutuality and sharing. The geometry of relation as expounded by Laing is diagramatised in living form in ritual.

If the private obsessions of individual neurotics are sublim-ated in corporate ceremonials, as the psychoanalysts maintain, this is because of a definite need for what Laing[16] calls 'a dialectical relationship to others' which is common to the race as a whole. It is in ritual that this dialectical relationship is most clearly seen – in small-scale rituals of the inter-personal acknowledgement of separateness and person-hood, in which the identity of the self is established, and in large-scale corporate rituals which serve the same function with regard to the community's own sense of identity. The formal inter-personal contact with the other afforded by ritual defines the limits of the body as identical with those of the self, and so reinforces the 'ontological security' of the self, its own identity in a viable reality. The body which is so limited and defined in corporate ritual is the community. It is the absence of such ritual, the inability to accept the challenge of otherness which accompanies any formalised meeting, any self-conscious encounter, which leads to estrangement and neurosis. We might therefore suggest that mankind has an instinct for ritual – and that it is the frustration of this instinct which is pathogenic. Private rituals, according to this hypothesis, are 'neurotic' simply *because they are private*. Their privacy is the cause as well as the expression of their wrongness. This would explain what Freud has such difficulty in explaining : the healthful and helpful quality of a phenomenon which reproduces the symptoms and, it is claimed, is rooted in the actual aetiology, of neurosis. If the purpose of ritual behaviour is to achieve contact with the other, then ritual which is not allowed to do this, because of a self-imposed privacy – in other words the indulgence of a private phantasy ritual which tries to make contact with a phantasied other – will bear all the marks of neurotic behaviour, behaviour which is 'unadaptive', and has no meaning in the real world of communicated and communicable experience. This ritual is the symbolic expression of a reality which is both individual and corporate, both psychological and societal. This reality is rooted in the individual psyche, but only finds its fulfilment in corporate action which is both self- and other-conscious. It is only unreal, only sick, only *neurotic*, when it is deprived of its fulfilment in an experience of belonging in a community of selves.

8. Ever since Freud stated that 'comparative research has been struck by the fatal resemblance between the religious ideas that we revere, and the mental products of primitive peoples and times', the practice among psychopathologists has been to make use of the religious rituals of 'primitive' societies in order to demonstrate the various stages of the psychological development of the individual. We might call this the 'explanation according to cultural psychopathology'. As we have already said, it is as much a reduction of social anthropology as of religion. Although it is concerned with whole societies and not with individuals, it antedates the work of the relationally-orientated writers we have been considering and goes straight back to the unitary approach of classical psychoanalysis. Where rituals are public and corporate they are treated as extensions of private rituals, and interpreted accordingly. In 'Childhood and Society', Erickson[22] makes use of the post-Freudian 'object-relations' hypothesis with regard to the origin of religious ritual, but extends it to include an explanation of the essentially corporate nature of such rituals, whereby information concerning the whole race is dramatised by 'a few exceptional individuals' in terms of their own aspirations and fears. In describing the religion of the Sioux Indians of North America, he demonstrates how the private 'consciousness of the culture's particular brand of inner damnation' is made public in order to produce a public katharsis, a shared expression and resolution of an essentially interior crisis. Here again the public ritual makes use of symbolic forms provided by the psychology and the rationally unacknowledged preoccupations of individuals with 'the paradise of orality, and its loss during the rages of the biting stages'.

In describing the religious ceremonies of the Yurok Indians, he says that 'the world image of the Yurok starkly suggests the oral mode of incorporation', the loss of the mother's breast, with its traumatic effect on the individual psyche, being reproduced in ritual form under the guise of 'the phylogenetic danger of possible loss of salmon supply from across the ocean'.

It is when present experience which is corporate or social relates to past experiences of an intra-psychic nature in the life of the developing individual, that it finds its expression in ritualistic religion. In its corporate, institutionalised form, however, this ritual behaviour is not considered neurotic, as it would be held to be in an adult individual.

According to Erickson, this is not because making a trauma public saves it from being neurotic or having a neurotic effect, but because the imagery of neurosis, by being universally intelligible on an unconscious level (as neuroses represent an inevitable stage in an individual's life-cycle), provides a convenient language for presenting significant and terrifying happenings in the outside world. Thus ritual is a language – but only when it has been severed from its roots in individual psychopathology, only when it has, so to speak, 'left home' and changed its real identity. Even then, its use as a language is confined to the area of magic and the performance of mighty acts in accordance with a homeopathic pattern of man's ability to influence his environment.

But surely this is a neurotic attitude to the outside world! Corporate ritual, as distinct from private obsessional behaviour, possesses 'homogenous cultural reality', but its reality is held to be magical and superstitious; what was not neurotic in the individual, being a normal part of human maturation, becomes neurotic in the race, as cultures strive ineffectively to change their environment by means of functional rites of manipulation and control. Thus, in effect, Freud is reversed, and we are left with an interpretation of corporate religion as concerned with objects rather than subjects – a kind of superstitious pseudo-science, which is actually quite different from the religion of moral aspiration and endeavour understood by Freud himself. Erickson accepts Durkheim's proposition that ritual constitutes a language employed by societies. Religious rites are 'a scenario whose purpose is communication'. The rite embodies a mythology which it uses as a means of transforming reality. But instead of a genuinely religious mythology with a religious purpose and effect it has a psychopathological scenario and is used for 'magical transformations'.

We should be careful to note, however, that Erickson is not saying that religious ritual is a neurotic regression to an infantile state, but that, just as magical thinking is proper to the individual psyche at a primitive and undeveloped stage of its maturational life, so corporate ritual illustrates in a graphic way the social thinking of a primitive society. Corporate rituals are primitive rather than neurotic; what would be neurotic behaviour in an adult person or a mature society is normal for children and savages; or at least for the incompletely civilised, whoever they may be.

When we remember how often we are confronted in our study of world religions by rites whose morphology, that is, their basic shape revolves around the figure of the womb and the idea of re-entry into a primal condition of existence, we can see how well the theory of neurosis as a recurrence of the infantile search for a 'lost object', the safe womb, the comforting breast, which is a need to regress into a condition of primal security, seems to fit as an explanation of religious rituals. And the fact that this original state of the individual psyche is regarded as a position not simply of security, but also of power, of complete autonomy – so that the infant experiences the environment as an extension of himself over which he has complete control, in which nourishment offers itself whenever he is hungry and goes away as soon as he is replete, and sensual satisfaction is total – certainly provides an attractive rationale of the rite's magical purpose.

But there are basic difficulties here. These concern, first of all, the necessity to explain the translation of an unconscious private fact into a conscious public concern. Erickson himself says that in order to establish what happens as a rite, as the vehicle of a conscious understanding about the existence of society, the rite's roots in the psychopathology of the individual have had to be broken. It has had to be externalised, made conscious, made corporate. Unconscious motives and blind drives have somehow been enabled to leap the gap into consciousness in order to provide a scenario for the expression of a powerful awareness of the facts of social life, to become a succinct message about 'the womb of social belonging'. Once we begin to talk in Erickson's terms about 'the phylogenetic womb of the race' as a concept which is understood and appreciated by the worshippers, we are beginning to countenance the conscious use of symbols, instead of the unconscious production of hysterical or neurotic symptoms, blind images of libidinal desires. We are in fact beginning to talk, not about depth-psychology, but about religion, about the contemplation of transcendental meaning and the striving to enter into relation with such meaning. In order to translate psychopathology into religion, Erickson has demonstrated that it is necessary to accept religion itself as an irreducible phenomenon!

Religious thinking, says Erickson, is a genuine thought-system; it is a constant and satisfactory way of organising our experience of the world. Satisfactory, that is, in terms of a recognisable stage in the psychological development of human beings and appropriate to that stage. But this is a primitive and immature stage in personal development, and religious rituals represent a way of behaving which belongs to primitive societies, to the 'childhood of the race'. We would note in passing that, for a primitive social phenomenon, womb symbolism, explicit symbols of rebirth into a new mode of life, a better, richer, higher mode than the one previously experienced, seems remarkably durable and persistent. It is by no means confined to 'backward' social organisations, and forms a vital part of the most developed religions, apart from recurring persistently in literature and art up to the present day. It may well 'reverberate in the unconsciousness', but it also speaks clearly to the adult consciousness, as a precise symbol of mortality and hope.

9. The link between the two kinds of ritual, interior and exterior, is to be found in the understanding of neurosis itself as a kind

of magical thinking.[17] All the same, ritual is acknowledged to be a mode of communication. Erickson's argument depends on establishing that, in the first place, the psychodynamics of neurotic thinking do in fact correspond to a belief in a magical potency implicit in these changes of mood which result from the dominance of 'the pressure of excessive wishes (the "id")' and 'the oppressive force of conscience (the "super-ego")'. Do these mood changes represent a way of coping with stress which commends itself to the neurotic individual as a way of avoiding the difficulties and angers of ego-directed consciousness – a way that is 'magical' in that it does not involve rational thought but lives directly in emotion and instinct? Or is this simply to make use of a cliché about religious ritual, that it is 'obviously' magical, to support a theory of neurosis? Freud certainly describes a neurotic conflict 'which is manifested in a change of mood from a vague conscious depression, through a certain in-between stage to heightened well-being and back'; but what is 'magical' about this? Indeed, there is reason to believe that the propositional, the scientific and non- or anti-magical powers of the psyche, which correspond to its ego functions, are exceptionally sharp during that part of the religious mood-swing which is characterised by 'heightened well-being'. Indeed, Maslow's[18] investigations into the quality of the religious 'peak-experience' have shown that the experiencing subject becomes aware at such times of a remarkable clarity of perception, in which all his faculties of thought and feeling appear to be sharpened to an abnormal degree. Far from the magical, the unexplained, he catches glimpses of a truth which explains many things that were previously quite obscure, an over-arching primary truth which provides the answer to the fundamental questioning of the rational intellect, without appearing to by-pass rationality.

[17] 'In psychoanalysis we think we have learned to understand something about this cycle (i.e. of sin and reparation, or 'usurpation and atonement') because we observe it again and again in individual histories.' C.f. also Freud, 'I am optimistic enough to suppose that mankind will surmount this neurotic phase just as so many children grow out of their similar neurosis.' *The Future of an Illusion*, p. 53.

This is the phenomenon originally described by William James in *The Varieties of Religious Experience*.[23] Dr Maslow's investigation into truly 'motiveless behaviour', behaviour which is not undertaken in order to satisfy primary instinctual urges and so achieve psychological homeostasis, reveals that such behaviour is very often the result of religious or artistic experience, which somehow leaves people free to act according to their own conscious choice. It is as though the cognitive and emotional barriers against such action were somehow dissolved by this kind of 'peak experience'. Maslow arrives at his conclusion through observation of people experiencing states of this kind. In particular we may note that the men and women who took part in his experiments bore witness to a feeling of freedom and reconciliation, a sense of being able to 'behave well'. Maslow comments that 'this finding, if it turns out to be correct, is in direct and flat contradiction to one of the basic axioms that guide all scientific (and philosophical) thought, namely, that the more objective and impersonal perception becomes, the more detached it becomes from value.' Religious experience, if it is truly religious, makes people feel and behave more maturely than they are otherwise capable of doing. Whatever depth-psychology might expect, religion turns out in practice to be more of a spring-board into the future than a bolt-hole into the past. It is associated with the ability to face new problems and to cope with life. Religious people, people of all religions, have always said this, of course. It is interesting to find psychologists agreeing with them.

It is surprising, however, how many contemporary psychologists are willing to take religion seriously. A. J. Ungersma, who is a follower of the 'existential psychologist' Frankl, asserts the existence of a religious sense which operates 'ab initio'; what Freud would have called a religious 'instinct', had he been willing to pay heed to such a possibility[18] – and not simply a

[18] 'After long doubts and vacillations, we have decided to assume the existence of only two basic instincts, Eros and the destructive instinct.' *The Outline of Psychoanalysis*, 1940. This seems to be Freud's last word on the subject.

function of repression, of the ego's disowning responsibility for some other instinct. This religious sense, says Frankl, may itself be repressed, with far-reaching behavioural consequences (c.f. Mowrer and the role of guilt feelings in the aetiology of neurosis). According to Freud's model, the unconscious is brought into the picture to redress the balance of consciousness, wherever the evidence provided by the latter is irrational or inconsistent. But the unconscious may equally well be held to mask an inherent awareness of divinity as the urge for free libidinal expression and satisfaction of the 'pleasure principle'. It is certainly true that the lacunae which so disturb us when life is viewed from the standpoint of a rational philosophy which is anthropocentric, fade into the background, and are somehow assimilated into existence as a whole, when we become aware of the actual and individual personhood of God, the God who is over against us and with whom we are in relation. The super-ego, says Freud, grows out of the ego's identification with a part of the external world; it is concerned, in the first place, with an extra-psychic reality or presence; the 'heir of the Oedipus Complex', it gains its force from the primal struggle of instinct with exterior prohibitions'. But the 'primal force' of the Oedipal situation may reflect a basic and powerful need for righteousness as obedience to an outside command, an exterior loyalty, which is not limiting but inspiring and inspiriting. Freud talks about 'residues of the super-ego in the id'; that is, in the unconscious itself. This certainly accords better with the positive evidence produced by investigation into religious 'peak experiences', such as that carried out by Abraham Maslow – and, originally, by William James. These times of heightened awareness present themselves as an expansion, even an explosion, of being rather than any kind of reduction or diminution: they are release and freedom, not control and repression. Indeed, they seem to represent the release of tensions and repressions which were previously unacknowledged, but which nevertheless exerted a powerful and destructive influence upon the personality.

If, as Mowrer and others have claimed, Freud was mistaken in maintaining that all the psychological determinants of human behaviour are to be sought for in the unconscious, we may pay just as much attention to, and attach equal significance to, periods of enriched and intensified consciousness, periods when the ego is most itself, most 'free', as to the unconscious sign-language of dreams. Indeed, for existential psychology, these 'peak-experiences' play the part of dreams in psychoanalysis. They are the 'place of truth', in which the psyche's original motivation, its basic message, becomes temporarily apparent. As with Freud, the exposure of hidden truth, hidden in the sense of being previously unrealised by and not incorporated in, the normal awareness, comes as an enrichment and a blessing. Maslow's investigations have shown that religious people are delivered from their everyday preoccupation with the cares and anxieties of life by an experience of heightened 'worthiness', of themselves and of the world and life in general; and that this kind of experience presents itself not as an homeostatic relief from tension, but as a positive access of power, a sense of enhanced *being*. And so we have evidence for our assertion that religious ritual, the self-conscious *celebration* of religious awareness, is the assertion of a precious truth about men and God, and not an attempt to placate a punitive deity in ways which are 'neurotic' and consequently meaningless.

10. However, we are primarily concerned here with an organised corporate phenomenon and not a private emotional response, whether this is held to be healthy and purposive or 'primitive' and 'neurotic'. Sociologically orientated writers and students of comparative religion protest strongly against the kind of argument which explains corporate ritual in terms of individual psychopathology. The world of ritual is the open world of social consciousness; it is not the enclosed world of the self's preoccupation with its own experiences, in which those involved are enabled to return to a primal bliss of complete personal

autonomy, 'I am the world and the world is me.' Corporate ritual is the embodiment of relationship-in-separation, the coming together of separate and distinct selves in their own limited and understood self-identity. As such it belongs to an entirely different way of being from the 'primary identification' of a child with its environment. Ritual which is corporate proclaims the mature self's victory over such infantile inclusionism. In a sense, the individual psyche provides itself in corporate rituals, with a new body, to become, during the duration of the rite, a new corporate person, someone who is his own relationship, his own otherness, a symbol of a mysterious unity and completeness. This new unity inevitably uses body symbolism to express itself; for this is what it is, a new body, a corporate maturity and wholeness, a humanised ideal; short-lived, perhaps, but attaining nonetheless a temporary perfection, a foretaste of a completeness which will be eternal. What is looked for here cannot possibly be achieved by any other kind of exercise than the rite, or by any demonstration of human skills or attributes which may be separated and distinguished from the flesh that gave them birth. Out of the ritualised commerce of bodies emerges the symbolic 'body' of society, the body of men in their essential interdependence, in their corporate holism. And because the rite makes use of men's bodies and the imagery of their bodily life, the social and religious becomes incorporated within the personal. A shared language allows a shared vision of things private and social. The body itself is seen as symbolising society. The common language of the corporal and the corporate, articulated in rituals of belonging, brings S. Paul to mind: 'we, being many, are one bread, one body, for we all partake of the one bread'.

The prevalence in corporate ritual of images drawn from the human body and its dispositions has been taken as evidence by anthropologists of the post-Freudian school that such rites reproduce the attitudes and feelings of infantile auto-eroticism.[19]

---

[19] 'We cannot possibly interpret rituals concerning excreta, breast milk, saliva and the rest unless we are prepared to see in the body a symbol of

But the body which is represented in corporate rituals, is essentially a consciously adopted symbol of freely given love towards other people, as distinct from the expression of the libidinal urge towards satisfaction at the hands of another person. It represents the desire of men and women to *belong together* so as to constitute one body, by taking it upon themselves to play separate and complementary roles in the life of the new corporate organism. The symbol is agapeutic, not erotic; again, we are reminded of S. Paul. This is not to suggest, however, that the human body's symbolism is not powerfully emotive or that it is altogether detached from the life of the unconscious.[20] Indeed, its conscious use in social and religious rituals is the most convincing proof that men take these rituals seriously. What better way could be found of expressing the importance attached by human beings to the vision of a real social belonging, to the understanding of human existence as essentially relational, and to their own resolve to give the vision and the understanding reality and form?

We are faced with the fact that, at no stage in its articulation does the 'explanation via psychoanalysis' really account for the corporate, the *related*, nature of religious ritual. Freud states quite plainly that obsessional behaviour always takes place in private; 'the presence of other persons during the performance of it is almost the participant's psyche, it is almost always out of the question'.[12] The rites of religion, on the other hand are essentially corporate. They express cultural values. They depict the world of men and objects and animals, the natural human environment. The mighty and terrible acts which they portray are mighty and terrible in outward reality, *social* reality, and not simply the externalisation of traumas, battles fought long ago in the individual participant's psyche. Eliade[24] calls them

---

society and to see the powers and dangers credited to social structure reproduced in small on the human body.' M. Douglas,[23] *Purity and Danger*, p. 115.

[20] 'Body symbolism is part of the common stock of symbols, deeply emotive because of the individual's experience ... Just as it is true that everything symbolises the body, so it is equally true that the body symbolises everything else.' M. Douglas, *Purity and Danger*, p. 122.

'the privileged expression of the existential situation' of societies. They are privileged in the sense of being both explicit
and ideal, the perfected statement of social truth, experienced
as primary truthfulness about man. 'This is all we can say,
but there is more to be said,' and so the rite is resonant with
expectation, and it is a religious resonance, a foretaste of future
blessedness and completion.

And so we come at last to the central issue in our discussion:
to what we might call the 'great divide' between scientific and
religious interpretations of religious phenomena. Scientific
explanations are reductionist: they *explain*, narrowing attention down from examples to principles. Religious thought is
expansionist, correlating data in order to enlarge its vision. In
a sense, religious thinking works backwards; it treasures the
evidence which points to what it already knows. Whereas
science sees problems as obstacles in the way of attaining truth,
as so many rivers to be crossed, and searches for stepping stones,
religion accepts the problem, plunges bodily into the river,
enjoys the river, welcoming it as part of a sanctified landscape
and adding it to its precious store of experiences which are
real and truthful. The data of the world and of experience
possess a final value for religious people, that they cannot
possess for those whose thinking is confined to scientific abstraction, however preoccupied science may be with examining and
comparing what it perceives and how it perceives it. Because
religion talks in symbols, religious thought has, in a sense,
already found what it is looking for. The thing itself, whatever
it may be, is symbolic of value and possesses meaning. It is
worthwhile for what it is *now*. Value streams back into it from
a conclusion which was its premise.

The mechanisms involved in ritual are symbolic of another
reality and point out a wider truth; whereas according to object-
relations theory the human body is ritually employed to
symbolise only itself. In other words, corporate ritual is not
really symbolic at all according to this reading, but a straightforward pictorial statement of a fundamental psychological

fact, the triumphs and tragedies of the pleasure principle.[21] The function of corporate ritual is much subtler and much more profound than this. C. G. Jung[25] has demonstrated that the intra-psychic language of the individual, the way he understands himself, is symbolic in the true sense, as it makes use of an archetypal symbolism which enshrines truths shared on an unconscious level, by the whole race. Whereas religious symbolism, as we understand it, is a conscious phenomenon. The function of corporate ritual is to bring these two symbolic languages, these two images of a wider truth, into alignment, and effectively to demonstrate that they do in fact belong together. The two kinds of symbol, the psychological and the cultural; the intra-psychic and the inter-psychic are equally valid, equally inevitable. But one is not simply to be reduced to the other. Religious homologisation stands over against scientific reduction. It is this homologisation, this demonstration of a valid parallel between inner and outer reality, that is one of the main purposes of corporate ritual, and that actually heals men. The question 'who am I, and where did I come from?' and the question 'who are *we*, and what is this world? – what is its purpose, what is its meaning?', are answered simultaneously and *in terms of each other*. Both man and his world are seen as having the same origin. Anthropogeny is described in terms of entogeny in order to express wholeness and belonging, unanimity, in the Creation. Man does not only project his own mythology on to nature, he takes a mythology from nature with which to interpret himself, and so he brings two worlds into relation. And so, as van Gennep[31] points out, rituals have a direct meaning, in the sense that what they portray is not secret, but a piece of precise information about the common life of society, that its peace and its health lie in its oneness with the universe. Rites reconcile man and his world – 'they show

---

[21] C.f. C. G. Jung.[25] 'I was on excellent terms with him (i.e. Freud), until I had the idea that certain things are symbolical. Freud would not agree to this and he identified his method with the theory, and the theory with the method.' 'That is impossible,' Jung remarks, 'you cannot identify a method with science.' *Analytical Psychology*, 1935, p. 140.

the world, not simply the image-making faculty of the individual psyche'.[31] We shall return to this theme later on, as it lies at the very heart of our argument.

At the centre of the corporate ritual act stands the individual human body, at once public and private, individual and corporate. The symbol points both ways, inwards and outwards, powerfully linking two worlds, the world of the person and the communal world of society, demonstrating their interdependence and mutual necessity, holding them together and allowing them to work as one reality.

11. To conclude then: Freud claims that religious ritual is closely linked to the private rituals of obsessional neurosis. This is apparent, he says, because of a close resemblance between the two kinds of ceremonial behaviour and also because of a supposed common aetiology in the Oedipal situation. Freud does not, or he cannot, explain why religious ritual is psychologically therapeutic, why one neurosis has the effect of alleviating the other; he mentions that this is indeed the case, but without explanation. We would suggest that religious ritual is in no sense neurotic, but rather the expression and realisation of a psychological truth about men in the world, and that the obsessional behaviour of neurotic people is pathological precisely because it represents a failed attempt to achieve the healthiness of inter-personal ritual behaviour, which healthiness is symbolised in corporate rituals. In fact, we would express the relation between private and public ritual thus: private ritual strives to reproduce on its own terms a reality which is essentially public, essentially corporate, which resists being included within the world of the self. We would say that the phantasied world of pseudo-relation in which the individual has dealings only with the various forms and manifestations of himself, stands over against the world of corporate experience, of the inter-relation of persons and things in an environment which owes its human viability to the quality of relation which subsists in it. Such a world is full of terrors for the sensitive, the

vulnerable, the introverted, the 'ontologically insecure',[16] but it is the world of authentic human experience, and somehow it must be entered and lived. The function of corporate ritual is to provide a means of entry into the world of relation, the world of the unknown other. The way is formal; it consists in a confession, which may be explicit or implicit (for the ritual act itself is just such a confession), of individual limitation and vulnerability, and a demonstration of corporate inter-dependence and inter-personal solidarity.

As Freud realised, strength comes from the truth, not from a lie; and corporate ritual is a confession and demonstration of the truth about men, their need for, and fear of, self-revelation in the presence of others. The courage to be among men con-sists in the courage to admit a reluctance to approach full inter-personal being; and it is the action of bringing weakness and insecurity into the light of the real world which encourages and reassures. It is the formal nature of the corporate action which proclaims its reality, its belonging to the actual world of communicable experience. The element of structure is treasured because it represents the distinctively *human* mode of communication. Ritual presents a 'third reality', distinct from the alternative realities of self and other. Its purpose is to demonstrate the embodied and concrete nature of human inter-personal experience as a counterpoise to meetings which are interior in the sense of being private. No meeting which is a genuine encounter with the other can remain private in the sense of not affecting the whole self and its overt behaviour in the world. We have already discussed the theological objec-tion to the erection of a structure for meeting otherness. Psychological objections would be found in a lack of courage or robustness which dare not declare itself, and so refuses the challenge of otherness, as this presents itself in the common environment of human beings, in other words, in Tillich's 'avoidance of being in order to avoid non-being'.[8]

On this showing, then, there is a world of difference, between ritual which is private and shared ritual, the difference between sickness and health. It does not seem useful, therefore, to classify religion as an obsessional neurosis simply because it involves ritual behaviour; and when we look closely at Freud we see that this is in fact what he is really doing.

12. But Freud's claim of a *special relation* between the two phenomena is supported by other writers who have dealt with the psychology of religion. Psychological health and the integration of personality are held to be closely involved with a sense of belonging in society; and society's own sense of itself, its corporate identity is similarly involved in its religious ceremonials. All religions, says Erickson, possess the insight that individual trust must become a common faith, and that the need for personal restoration must become a part of the practice of the whole community. We might also point out that, in itself, the connection between religion and fatherhood need not be the negative one suggested in *The Future of an Illusion*. Parents are not simply objects of ambivalent feelings of love and hatred who must always be placated. Even within the Freudian system they play an enabling role in the process of psychological maturation through identification. This role is reinforced by religious ritual which plays its part in fostering the self-hood and sense of identity of the growing child through its demonstration of a 'hierarchy of social positions'. Also, a sense of relationship and inter-dependence. For a growing child, ritual is a way of establishing the known and dealing with the unknown, formally, realistically (i.e. not in fantasy) and in company with others. It is a way of growing. The life of the intellect and the emotions is explored in the real world among real people; it is not kept hidden away to be developed as a thing apart, the individual person's private concern, an unseen limb, which shares the properties of omnipotence and invulnerability.

Jung, in *Psychology and Religion*,[25] comes out quite definitely on the side of formal religion as a source of mental and spiritual health, and a way of coming to terms with the life of the unconscious. Ritual is 'the crystallized form of original religious experience'. Its function, which is also its justification, is to safeguard the individual consciousness from 'the full force of the collective unconscious', by channelling this into symbolic shapes which can be contemplated without terror, yet serve to enrich the personality through contact with the creative depths of its own psychic being. Thus religion communicates a healing and inspiring power drawn from 'the ancient rituals of the creation, ceaselessly renewed in the collective unconscious'. Thus Jung is allied to those writers who regard religion as social truth rather than as a kind of corporate error (e.g. Freud, Marx). The Jungian concept of the 'collective unconscious' counters the personalist Freudian stress and encourages us to regard public rituals as a manifestation of, and an encouragement to, a healthful self-identity. Jung argues in favour of rituals in which the element of the unknown, and the suggestion of the unknowable, are boldly faced and not in any way vitiated by explanations. For it is not an intellectual understanding which is acted out in religious ritual, but a sense of the limitations imposed on such cognition. The archetypal symbolic forms which emerge in them are at once meaningful and opaque. They are a groping after a truth which concerns the whole race. The action of searching for the collective truth about mankind communicates something of that truth, if it is allowed to do so, without the interposition of a preconceived intellectual understanding.

The effect of a corporate ritual which allows itself to be symbolic in a true sense, that is, to point beyond itself towards a reality that defies propositions, an underlying reality and truth, is to make that reality and that truth in some sense and to some degree available to those who participate in it. This is a learning process, in which we are taught how to exist by learning about being. It is learning *through* involvement *about* involvement, learning about the unanalysable totality by being immersed in the experience of that totality. The symbolic forms which find expression in such rituals have what Jung calls 'an alchemical effect' – they transform ordinary reality into something infinitely more precious.

Not all psychologists, then, interpret corporate rituals in the light of the obsessional behaviour of neurotic people. They would agree that religion is not a disease but the cure for a disease, and ritual is the application of the cure.

C. Ritual and Anthropology

If Calvin is the key-figure in the theological attack on ritual as 'unspiritual' and 'idolatrous', and Freud the leader of all those who regard ritual as 'neurotic' or 'infantile', then Frazer[26] is the authority who is most responsible for the widespread contempt for corporate ritual as the sign of a world-view which is 'magical' and 'primitive'. In *The Golden Bough* he puts forward the suggestion that religion is the second of three stages in the development of human culture. It is preceded by magic and followed by science. In his enterprise of subjugating the natural world, man first of all turned his attention to the homology of phenomena, and *homeopathic magic* emerged; next, he postulated the presence of spirit helpers who possessed invisible techniques of transformation of people and objects, and could be induced to put these techniques at the disposal of men; last of all – and this last stage corresponds to full racial maturity – man learnt by observation how to figure out for himself how things work, and consequently how he might make them work for him. All three stages are seen as part of the process whereby mankind has grown into the functional mastery of his environment. Magic represents 'the immediate expression of man's need and desire to control the forces of his environment whilst as yet he knows nothing of their nature'.[26] Religion and its rituals are a development of magic, with its spells and incantations; but both religion and magic belong in intention to science. With religion and magic, however, the intention fails; only in science does mankind finally win the mastery.

1. According to this view the purpose of religious ritual is functional, and it is a practical way of changing one set of circumstances into another through the agency of men skilled in a specific technique. It is important to remember that the traditional Judaeo–Christian acceptance of ritual worship only differs from this in ascribing the principle agency to God – it is God who uses the ritual forms and techniques to change the situation for men. Ritual is still functional, but it is, in the first place at least, God who functions, and his way of functioning is *theologically explained*. It is this explanation, which, in the eyes of Christians, removes the stigma of magicality from the sacrament. (Hence the Christian stress upon doctrine and myth at the expense of ritual action.) And indeed, there is an important difference between these two kinds of actions, actions done by men, and actions done by men in the belief that their efficacy is not human in any reducible sense, but proceeds from elsewhere. Only the second kind of action can be called any sort of a religious rite. To describe such rituals as a kind of science, as straightforward propositional exercises in manipulating known quantities, is simply not adequate.

The work of Bronislaw Malinowski[27] demonstrates the limitations of Frazer's views, and establishes once and for all that even the simplest religious rite has an entirely different function from any kind of scientific technique, however rudimentary. The two forms of behaviour, religious and scientific, fulfil different social needs; success and failure in either is judged by entirely different criteria. 'Magic (is defined) as a practical art consisting of acts which are only means to a definite end expected to follow later on.' Magic, then, is functionally like science. But religion is always 'a body of self-contained acts being themselves the fulfilment of their purpose'. Ritual satisfies existential needs, science answers rational questions.

However, although the function of religion differs from that of magic, on the one hand, and scientific enquiry, on the other, religion is still primarily functional. 'Since we cannot define cult and creed by their objects, perhaps it will be possible to define their function.' The variety of the religious systems evolved by different cultures leads, not to an understanding of religion as a basic phenomenon, possessing many forms or expressions, but to an 'explanation' of religion as a function of something else, in this case society. By asserting a positive re-action to the forces of social entropy at certain crisis-periods in the life of the community, religion fulfils a vital social func-tion. Malinowski sees the rite as a social tool, having its most typical expression in mortuary rituals, when society, faced with the threat of destruction as this is symbolised by the actual death of one of its members, consciously selects the positive option of religious hope in the face of personal despair and social disintegration. However, it would be true to say that this theme of 'life-out-of-death' actually underlies all religious thinking (and not only the religious thinking of primitive peoples, as Frazer concluded). It occurs spontaneously at times of crisis, and is particularly associated with those times, be-cause they are times when the search for newness, and the reaching out towards possibility, are at their highest pitch. But this search, and this reaching out, are ever-present within the life of man. They do not simply fulfil a function for man, but are inextricable from his very being. They are *his* function. That their perfect expression can only proceed from a death, the death of whatever has gone before, whatever was previously possible but is now seen to be inadequate for the new situation, is signified by the importation of some kind of symbolic death into every religious ritual. Thus the specific death-situation does not use religion as a means to an end, but religion demonstrates its hopeful truth by using the potent image of death-and-resurrection. Malinowski has confused the purpose of religious faith, the expression of solidarity with divinity, with its re-sult, the assertion of social solidarity. This having been said, however, the fact remains that there is certainly no tendency here to confuse the expressive role played by religious ritual with the directly functional, in the sense of instrumental, in-tention of science or of magic. Malinowski, says Talcott Parsons, 'shows quite clearly that neither ritual practices, magical or religious, nor the beliefs about supernatural forces and entities integrated with them, can be treated simply as a primitive and inadequate form of rational techniques of scientific knowledge; they are qualitatively distinct, and have quite different functional significance in the system of action'.[29]

2. If Malinowski draws attention to the difference between the social function of scientific procedures and religious ceremonies, Durkheim and his followers establish the mutual exclusiveness of these two kinds of social action. The distinguishing mark of religious ritual as against scientific technique is that the former is without any direct utilitarian purpose at all. Religion and its rites, says Durkheim, cannot be considered to be functional, for the sacred does not initiate anything so much as it celebrates or demonstrates something. A rite is a symbolic action which expresses aspiration; it expresses it as faith – insofar as that what is asked for is experienced as being, in a symbolic sense, already present. The world has *really* been changed before the rite begins. The rite proclaims the accession of meaning into the environment of the believer. It is 'radically dissociated from any utilitarian context'.[28] In the process, it alters reality indirectly, by affecting feelings and attitudes. But it sets out to do something quite different – to express religious *belonging*.

Thus there is present in Durkheim's writing a genuinely sociological acceptance of religion. It is not only that religion is concerned with, and addresses itself to, society as a whole, and expresses the values of the community rather than having as its main purpose the satisfaction of the emotional or practical needs of individuals (which had already been pointed out by Robertson Smith): but that social needs and intentions are at last recognised as being qualitative different from the needs and intentions of individual people. Societies, in other words, are not to be regarded as simply the sum of the individuals who comprise them. Societies are structured for strength and adaptability in the face of the individual's weakness and rigidity; they are organised for majority survival in the face of individual selfishness and inefficiency. They have a life of their own, powers – and weaknesses – of their own. In all this, says Durkheim, religion plays a leading, if not *the* leading, part. Religion is concerned with making a group of individual people into a community, with providing the behavioural norms which form the backbone of society, giving it its distinctive shape – allowing it to have any shape at all. Religion is no more the sum of men's conscious desires, needs, fears, as the 'functionalist' writers claimed, than it is of their unconscious ones, as Freudian anthropology asserts. Religion speaks to men about society; about common needs, common interests and concerns, strengths and weaknesses; and in so doing it helps society to be itself, to arm itself against the violent reaction of individualism. It encourages the formation of families and family groupings; more than this even, it builds itself on to the social system and becomes the medium of the system's own articulation, its channel of interior communication, the very language of the individual's and the family's commitment to the wider family and more robust individuality represented by the community.

To writers of this 'structuralist' persuasion, social rules and the rites of religion are very closely allied; indeed, they are almost the same thing. Rites, says Durkheim, are 'the rules of social conduct which prescribe how a man should comport himself in the presence of sacred objects',[28] – and religion is 'a unified system of beliefs and practices relative to sacred things'. But the sacred thing is, in fact, society itself, or at least society in its ideal form, that ideal society to which real society aspires, the inspirational society of the future. We can see now how religion and its rites both express the character of a particular society, its essential 'shape', and also serve to perpetuate and strengthen that character and shape. The process is a circular one. It is in religion that society expresses its sense of identity as society rather than as merely an ad hoc collection of individuals; it is in religious *ritual* that it demonstrates this

self-consciousness to itself and to others, and thereby strengthens and enriches the experience of corporate self-hood which
emerges as social action. The rites of religion serve to externalise the truth about a society, the facts of its corporate life,
by demonstrating the corporate nature of that life in symbolic
form. In this way ritual allows societies to recognise themselves, to embrace their own distinctive identity, to 'catch up
with themselves'.[22] In religious ritual men take stock of the
unseen truths which direct and inspire their lives, and discover
them to be truths about inter-dependence and relationship.
Thus, there is no suggestion in Durkheim's analysis that religion is a creation of social systems; just the opposite – social
systems are established, strengthened, and directed by considerations which are religious. 'The ideal society presupposes
religion, far from explaining it,' for 'society is above all the
idea which it forms of itself'.[28] What is expressed in religion
is not society as it is, but society as it might be; or as it is
potentially. Ritual reveals to us an ideal society, which represents the collective aspirations of the community. The moral
sentiments and ideas which emerge from ritual in the form of
a conceptualised self-identity are fed back into the social system which produces and lives in it. The effect of ritual is to
bridge the gap between ideas and things. Feelings and attitudes
become associated with those actions and objects used to represent them. The result is that, on the one hand, 'collective sentiments acquire a sort of physical nature',[28] while on the other,
nature itself becomes infused with meaning, and man is im-
pressed with the knowledge of his social identity by means of
the vision vouchsafed him of an ideal existence in a harmony
of nature and human society which is total and complete. Thus,
in ritual, 'the individual learns to idealise ... and in idealisa-
tion society creates itself'.[28] Ritual is thus the way in which
society demonstrates itself to itself; rites are employed to es-

[22] 'It is by common action that (society) takes consciousness of itself and
realises its position ... the collective ideas and sentiments are even possible
only owing to these exterior movements (of the rite) which symbolise them.'
E. Durkheim, *The Social Foundations of Religion*, 1913.

tablish the social meaning and significance of existential truth – which is the truth of relation, of corporate belonging, the religious truth which transcends self to reach out to the other in his otherness. 'Religion,' says Durkheim, 'should be an eminently collective thing.'

3. Religious ritual then is not, in Durkheim's view, 'magical', and, of course we agree with him. The primary purpose of the rite is not to change reality by means of a technique, but to enjoy reality as it is, or as it is in ideality; by which we mean the reality which underlies everyday reality, and gives it meaning and direction:[23] Ritual which is authentically religious concerns itself with the known, and, in a mythical sense, the understood. It expresses a corporate or social understanding about people and about life. There is no deception here. Those who take part are 'in on what is going on'. To outsiders, those who do not belong to the community, the rite may appear secret, but to those taking part it is an 'open secret', a happening whose meaningfulness and significance is shared by all. This is quite different from the kind of rite described by Frazer,[26] the essence of which lies in its exclusiveness and absence of sharing. The 'magical' rites described in *The Golden Bough* almost always invoke knowledge which is withheld from those partaking in the rite, and remains the closely guarded property of the shaman or priest.[24] The rites are magical because they are not explained. Frazer argues that they are not, in fact, explicable, for they are a kind of trick involving sleight of hand, in which the desired effect is counterfeited and a substitute passed as a reality, by men who are too naïve, both deceivers and deceived, really to know the difference between fact and fiction. Frazer, like Freud, takes no account at all of symbolism

[23] C.f. Jardine Grisbrooke – 'Liturgy is common acts done in an uncommon way with uncommon significance, in order to restore that significance to all common acts.'

[24] 'The noise [which accompanies the ceremonial "death" in the ritual of a particular tribe] is made with bamboo trumpets, but the women and children think it is made by the devils, and are much terrified.' J. Frazer, *The Golden Bough.*

in ritual, of the sign that 'partakes in that to which it points', and so changes reality by changing men's emotions and attitudes; he only knows a way of using ritual in an attempt to change reality instrumentally.[25] The implication in all the descriptions of initiatory rites in *The Golden Bough* is that those who undergo them are simply unaware of the figurative nature of the proceedings, and believe the miraculous to be really happening and the forces of nature to be obediently responding to the address of men. The essence of the rite is deception.

The mechanism of these 'magical' rites, may be clearly distinguished from the myths in which they are decked out. But in symbolic ritual, the action of the ritual is one with its subject matter, and the effect lives within the story, working by *poetical* means involving psychological forces of imagination and identification. With Frazer, however, the action of the ritual is authentically scientific and may be explained propositionally. Just as, according to Freudian anthropology, a neurotic person draws upon his own unconscious mind in order to make use of techniques acquired in childhood to change his own personal reality, so the Frazerian shaman gains access to an unseen world inhabited by spiritual beings who are bound to do his bidding with regard to a reality which is public, the affairs of the community as a whole. The myth provides a framework for the magical process, but is not itself that process. It also *seems* to explain it – that is, the miraculous events of the myth which belong to the fabled past of the tribe seem to be taking place in the present, and the uninitiated are led to believe that this is indeed the case. The myth is in fact used to give those taking part in the rite an impression of a 'homeopathic' transformation of the real into its ideal or mythical counterpart. This, however, is a kind of smoke screen which

[25] In describing the death and resurrection rituals of 'primitive' races, in which young men are 'killed' and 'restored' mimetically in order to revitalise the whole tribe, Frazer says that 'such rites become intelligible if we suppose that their substance consists in extracting the youth's soul in order to transfer it to his totem. His recovery would be attributed to the infusion into him of fresh life drawn from the totem.' *The Golden Bough*, p. 691.

disguises the real nature of the proceedings, which are *not* explained, although, as we have seen Frazer attempts to explain them. He is most concerned to demonstrate that primitive ritual can be explained 'rationally' and 'scientifically'. If the process is 'unscientific', this is because those who manipulate it are bad scientists in that their reasoning is based on a faulty premiss, the actual existence of a spirit world which obeys the same natural laws as the world of everyday reality, and is in fact a recognisable part of that world; but they are, according to their own lights, still scientists for all that, and they employ mythical forms only in order to add an extra force to their scientific attempts to change reality.

'Sacramental' myths, which are understood by those who participate in them to hold in themselves the power to change reality in ways which are not subject to scientific analysis, do not enter into Frazer's thinking at all. Like Freud, he 'concretises' spiritual reality. The Christian understanding of a myth which 'explains' poetically and figuratively, and is accepted as the *only* explanation of the ritual which embodies it, is much closer to the anthropological thinking of Malinowski[27] and Durkheim.[28] Such myths are the symbolic representations of an underlying reality which is itself the source and the object of meaning – that is, they are religious symbols, not simply because their mythical form concerns itself with gods and their actions and intentions, but because the understanding of society which underlies the myth and causes it to emerge is experienced as a religious reality.

4. Ritual, then, is a social language, with a social meaning. It speaks to society about society. More than this, it is *religion*, religion sui generis and not any kind of 'primitive' natural science. This principle, asserted first of all by Robertson-Smith[30] and articulated by Durkheim, is given further definition by the investigations carried out by van Gennep[31] into the morphology of existing rituals. The model laid down in *Les Rites de Passage* has proved seminal for later anthropol-

ogists. According to this model, principal crises in the life-cycle of each individual member of a society – beginning with birth and passing through puberty to marriage, parenthood and death – are marked by rituals, the significance of which, although they they have a deep and lasting effect upon the inner life of the person concerned is primarily social. The individual is reached and inspirited through the symbolism of society, the understanding of corporate belonging. What we are presented with is a succession of initiatory scenarios, each of which has the effect of incorporating the individual or group of individuals, concerned into a new position within the social framework. The purpose of corporate ritual, says van Gennep, is incorporation within a defined social status.[26] This is not automatic or inevitable – it is not simply to be equated with a maturational stage attained by an individual – but is accorded to a member of a society in and through a definite ritual, the particular purpose of which is to overcome specific difficulties or problems, which are the inevitable *interpersonal* problems and difficulties entailed in any kind of social organisation. Here, again, ritual is seen as a public meeting aimed at reconciliation and mutuality, an 'official' form given to a necessary encounter. This is why the notion of a ceremonial meal occurs so often in anthropologists' accounts of religious rituals; the meeting of man and man, and man and God, is recognised as involving powerful ideas of differentiation and opposition, both essential and existential. Van Gennep's followers have pointed out that the rite serves to codify corporate existence, existence within society, in that the dialectical element in relationship is expressed and accommodated within it. Religion becomes a unifying factor, not simply the expression of an existing unity as Durkheim concluded. Max Gluckman[32] sees the main function of ritual as cloaking the fundamental conflicts set up 'where there is a confusion of roles and relationships within

---

[26] 'The rituals which Frazer saw as fruits of mental processes and ideas are in fact to be understood on terms of the social relations which are involved in the rituals.' Max Gluckman, *The Ritual of Social Relationships*, p. 24.

a closed society, with the corresponding tensions and ambiguities that such a situation involves'.[27] Indeed, we have already remarked on the ambivalence of religious ritual – the tendency for rites to be about existential discords, and 'impossible possibilities'. If, as Durkheim maintains (and as is generally agreed), ritual expresses an 'ideal' situation, and contributes to its attainment in reality, existing ambivalence cannot simply be ignored. It must be shown rather to be capable of being triumphantly resolved. In and through the religious consciousness embodied in the ritual 'code' difficulties and conflicts are presented as being overcome in a specialised ritual relation of reconciliation.

Ritual, then, asserts and establishes social truth, truth about social obligations and expectations, social relationships, by public performance of an ideal social message, a message which is ideal in its acceptance and transcendence of existing truth rather than its choice of an alternative reality. Rites, says Fortes, 'function in order to overcome cleavages on society'.[28] But in order to do this, they must be concerned not with deception, but with the revelation of social truthfulness.[29] All this, of course, proceeds from Durkheim's recognition of the function of religious ceremonial in proclaiming what society knows to be true about itself and about its way of being in the world; but van Gennep's revelation of the *direct social meaning of the rite*, its explicit purpose as a means of welding individuals into society by providing them with an institutionalised way of coping with existential stress, a means of support and reassurance during identity-crises, certainly counters the Frazerian assertion that ritual's aim is to change outward reality by

---

[27] 'What Durkheim missed when he derived "God" from the feeling of the pressure of society at an Australian corroborree was that the members of the congregation assembled in unity there were enemies of one another in many other situations.' M. Gluckman, op. cit.

[28] Fortes draws special attention to the role of mortuary rites in reconciling warring family interests among the Yako (quoted in Gluckman).

[29] In his study of Ndembu circumcision ritual, in Gluckman's book, V. W. Turner draws attention to 'the value the Ndembu set on making things visible, open and true, on public knowledge rather than private secrecy'.

inward means. The truth according to van Gennep turns out to be quite the opposite. As we shall see later on, van Gennep's 'homeopathy' which is really the religious homology of man and nature, 'homeopathy' in reverse, tells us much more about the life of man in a world which he experiences as 'other', emphatically not himself, than any anthropocentric 'explanation' of rites which denies their intrinsic symbolism. The shape of ritual, its recurring and consistent tri-partite form, which van Gennep refers to as the division into 'preliminal', 'liminal', and 'post-liminal' rites (from the Latin *limen*, a doorway), only really makes sense as religion or social theory in accordance with the Durkheimian homologisation of social and religious belief. The rite is always some kind of initiation into a fuller and more complete way of being, whether this is seen from an explicitly religious standpoint, as with Eliade, or from a sociological one. Van Gennep resolutely refuses to isolate and explain symbols apart from their significance in the social process. We might comment that the symbolic language of the 'rites of passage' expresses the need to join man to his environment by demonstrating a natural link between the life of man and the life of the world, not to tame the world by pretending that it is a projection of man's psyche, and so subject to his whims.

5. Would it be true, then, to say that all corporate rituals are religious, in the Durkheimian sense of asserting the spiritual solidarity of the community? Or can some rites reasonably be regarded as magical in intention? What in fact is a magical rite? Neither van Gennep, nor Durkheim himself is able to answer this question in a way that provides us with a satisfactory alternative to the explanation given by Frazer that *all* religious rites are magical, in that they are attempts to change the environment by 'homeopathic science'. According to Frazer, magic is causality which cannot be explained by natural science. Van Gennep, having explained the social origin and effect of corporate rituals, goes no further. The mythological dress in which these rituals are clothed is still assumed to be a straight-for-

wardly homeopathic attempt to transform natural situations into ideal ones by applying appropriate techniques of manipulation. The rites remain inexplicable, in the sense that the explanation offered by those taking part, explanation, that is, in terms of the myth, is obviously unscientific. It is therefore assumed to be magical. That is to say, van Gennep is content to separate the *effect* of the initiatory rite, its role in structuring, creating, and re-inforcing society, from its *purpose*, the intention of those taking part in it, which is taken to be the magical transformation of nature, both human and otherwise. It is a way of changing men into gods or heroes, or of enduring them with the characteristics of certain favoured or admired animals. Thus the rite itself is a tool for reproducing mythical events. The myth is intended as the rationale of the rite. Of course, it certainly would not convince more mature and sophisticated societies; it therefore follows that the rite is the sign of primitive thinking and social organisation.

But this constitutes a retreat from the structuralist position set out by Durkheim; the rite is on no account to be considered functionally, as a kind of tool; it is rather a symbolic language, inducing courage, devotion, and skill in the worshippers, so that they are inspired to transcend themselves as individuals sharing in the race's ritual super-identity. As long as the real significance of the myth is misunderstood or overlooked, the problem of magic remains. Myth and rite belong together – so much is axiomatic. Both myth and rite are the expression of an existential crisis, an unavoidable religious awareness that must be recognised in symbolic action. The rite is the crisis as it is felt, the myth the crisis as it renders itself capable of being *thought*. The myth does not explain the rite in the sense of proceeding from it, standing over against it as a kind of commentary on it; it lives within the rite, articulating the rite's meaning and purpose, giving the rite actuality as a happening in the present by endowing it with the authority of a saving event in 'mythical history', that is history seen through the eyes of religious faith, from which event it is *indistinguishable*. Each rite is 'explicable' only in terms of its mythology, even as the myth itself cannot be separated from its enactment and emerges from a ritual scenario of things too deep for words, of the irrational and unarguable movements of the soul.

If we define magic as 'that which is inexplicable in terms of scientific causality', there must always be something magical about corporate ritual. We are accustomed to thinking scientifically; religious ritual demands that we break the habit, and think theologically; that is, within the rite's own thought system. If we would understand ritual, we must learn not to impose upon it a code of meaning which is alien to it, which is, as it were imported from outside. Science views religion and its manifestations according to its own image, and regards everything which refuses to succumb to its techniques as 'magical' and 'primitive'. But religion will not yield its unique meaning to any other way of thinking about reality. Religious thought, mythic thinking, co-ordinates heterogeneous elements, contains within itself logical contradictions, makes a statement about mutually exclusive ideas, Gods and men, power and weakness, the uncaused and the caused. It conceptualises a dialectical experience of union and diversity, relationship in separation. It accepts and accommodates scientific nonsense in the light of its knowledge of a higher and completer science.

For this reason, scientific explanations of ritual always stop short of completeness. They employ the wrong system of explanation – not totally wrong, but not right enough, not comprehensive enough. Certainly it is true to say that some rites, and some parts of most rites, may be explained naturalistically in terms of their usefulness in placating or persuading or imitating; but the essence of the rite always escapes such analysis. The rite is neither description nor measurement. It is not even discourse. It is dialogue, or more precisely, conversation, an endless dialogue, an inconceivable conversation. Thus it is dynamic; it cannot be extrapolated for purposes of examination without destroying its life and making something quite different out of it. It is no kind of blueprint. What it says, it says in the form of address, for its purpose is meeting and communion. Above all, the rite is being, not doing. For what men do in the rite, they do in order to show what they are, rather than to establish what they are capable of performing. Included in the rite is the acknowledgement of naturalistic causality and scientific techniques, the awareness of the rules of survival 'in the world'; but the specifically religious value of the rite is always to be found elsewhere. Indeed, it is located just at the point where scientific explanation stops short, and reason is rebuked.

The rite possesses all the properties of language. It uses logic to express the illogical or the supra-logical. In itself it is never a mere formula, because it is capable of pointing the way to what cannot be formulated. Its principle is flexibility and expressiveness; it contains within itself the possibility of precision, but it is more than this possibility. An experience which, in its transforming power may have an unforgettable impact, remains vague and evocative, full of surprises, inspirational. Only in this way is it able to open up new kinds of truth, new ways of knowing. The rite's similarity to scientific procedure is a confusing irrelevance, born of our modern Western preoccupation with verbal and written communication and neglect of the language of gesture. It is assumed that organised corporate activity must be functional rather than expressive. It is an unwarrantable assumption. As far as ritual is concerned the truth is just the reverse. The rite exists in order to tell us about the limitations of the ability of natural science and logical reasoning to provide us with an adequate language for human existence.

6. For van Gennep and Durkheim, then, as for Frazer himself, the magical is 'that which is inexplicable in terms of the system'. But the system, unfortunately, is imposed rather than induced. Like van Gennep, Durkheim misses the essential co-inherence of rite and myth, their synchronicity. He regards myth as, quite simply, the explanation of rite, in the sense that

he is able to explain most rites as contributing to a social purpose which may be distinguished as present in the myth. But
whenever the social purpose of myth and rite is not clear, he
too falls back on the notion of magic. In actual fact, of course,
as we have said above, the myth *always* has a social purpose,
in that it provides an over-arching truthfulness which is able
to relate contrary elements – positive and negative, purpose-
less and purposeful, productive and sterile – within a single
universe, a single socio-religious system. Ritual demonstrates
and embodies a completeness which can be understood only as
a religious phenomena, in religious terms. Myth and rite present the whole picture of man's life in the world in a way that
makes sense to those involved in it. The picture is necessarily
an idealised one, because, outside this ritual universe and the
religious awareness that it expresses, the world remains existen-
tially unintelligible, or at least disturbingly inconsistent. If in
and through the rite 'society learns to idealise',[28] this is because it learns there to contemplate existential discords. The clue
to this lies, not in the reasonableness of the myth as an explanation of the rite, but in its unintelligibility on anything other
than an ideal plane. The myth demonstrates the rite as ideal
truth, as religion. Because he does not really accept the theological nature of ritual, its consistency as a dialectical system,
Durkheim cannot widen his understanding of rituals enough to
include all corporate rites. The true nature of some rites, their
place within the system of ritual, still eludes him. He is forced
back on Robertson-Smith's division of corporate rituals into
two separate categories, those which are understood to serve
a social purpose, and those which are not so understood. For
these latter, some other explanation must be found.

7. A useful explanation lies ready to hand in the notion of *social
hygiene*. Not all corporate rites are symbolic of social processes and therefore deserve to be called religious because of the
sacred quality attaching to such processes; some ceremonies
are merely ways of avoiding actions or objects which are

counted as dangerous because they are unclean or impure. Such rituals aim at avoiding defilement, not sacrilege. Because they are irrational and do not lend themselves easily to explanation in terms of any social reality, these 'hygienic' acts are still called magical. They exist outside the system.

In her book *Purity and Danger*, Mary Douglas[23] points out that Durkheim's view of society is an over-simplified one. Social systems are altogether more complex than he allowed. Dr Douglas is not willing to allow any kind of 'magical causality' to remain within social theory. Within the code of symbolism employed by society, the negative as well as the positive may be contained, indeed *must* be contained. Every social rule, even those which seem to be a magical protection against uncleanness, contributes to the structuring of society, and carries its 'load of social symbolism'.

That our religious feelings are in a very deep sense interconnected with ideas about the conditions of our corporate, racial, tribal, sectarian, identity is, since Durkheim, widely accepted. Dr Douglas points out in extension of this that the conditions which establish corporate self-hood are also defences against any infringement of the area of experience that they establish as belonging to the race, tribe, or sect. We cherish certain ideas and classifications because they define the terms of our corporate identity, that is, because they define *us*. Our religious rules are the conceptual expression of what Tillich has called 'our courage to be as a part'. That which defiles is nothing else than that which does not fit our tribal classification system, our picture of the ideal society; 'our pollution behaviour is the reaction which condemns any object or idea likely to confuse or contradict cherished classification'.

8. Neurotic people are also concerned with questions of ordering and classification and this is considered to be symptomatic of their specific kind of alienation from 'the normal'. Is Mary Douglas lending support here to the Freudian thesis which says that religious ritual is the result of a religious 'neurosis'? Not

necessarily. When we were talking about neurotic behaviour we allowed for the existence of an 'instinct for ritual' which demands satisfaction. We can now expand this by saying that this is really a need for symbolic expression of the instinct for social being and belonging. The private, inward-looking rituals of the neurotic proceed from an urgent need to give formal expression to a truth about the self in a situation which seems opposed to both the expression and the truth. The truth is about relationship, the need for contact with the other, in action with other people. Thus truth and expression are one, for such a truth is not to be separated from the actions which express and embody it – hence the need for exteriorisation, for a formal presentation of something which is not an idea, to be entertained privately and secretly, but an event, a happening, which in order to be experienced must be enacted. If, however, circumstances are against such an enactment (which makes use of the total environment, other objects, other circumstances, other people and their attitudes, motives, capabilities, etc.), alternative circumstances may always be substituted by the power of the human imagination, and the happening may proceed with a fantasy 'cast' in the secrecy of the chief actor's own mind.

Since the truth about the self which seeks expression in neurotic ritual is a social truth, it cannot help involving a concept of society and the relation of the self to existing social forms. Laing[18] describes an experience of the insecure and vulnerable psyche in the presence of other individuals who are felt to be a source of threat; might we not consider the effect on the 'ontologically insecure' of an insupportable societal experience, an apprehension of society itself as a menace? Social concerns express themselves in ritual forms; a pathological ritual may well signify a maladjustment which is social, a condition of the individual's relationship with a total environment. It may represent a statement about a social reality which is felt to be malstructured, or not adequately structured, or overstructured. The reduction of corporate ritual to ritual which is secret and concerns only the self, might reveal a desire to cut oneself off from membership of the real society, and to create a kind of private fantasied social belonging in order to preserve the illusion of authenticity. Such an enterprise is bound to involve a parallel system of rules of social interaction, a similar ordering of corporate experience to that existing in the real world. Society is experienced as having a certain shape. This shape is governed by rituals which serve to delineate its boundaries. The rituals have a dual purpose as symbols, for they draw attention both to what is included in the society, and to what is excluded from it. Certain objects and actions belong inside society and are acceptable; certain other objects and actions belong outside society and are to be shunned by its members. This preoccupation with frontiers would seem to correspond to that need to define and delineate, to categorise and to tabulate, which is a characteristic of the pathologically alienated. The difference is that one is public and concerned with the relation of otherness and the principles governing the interaction of separate and distinct selves, and the other is private and concerned with the inclusion of alien phenomena within the self. One is concerned with asserting boundaries and establishing differences, and the other with homogenising experience and denying all otherness and difference. One is concerned with life in the world and the public actions and inventions of men, and the other with an illusory substitute for such actions and inventions, a trick to deceive both others and the self.

Durkheim associates the magical with the unclean, and leaves them both outside the mainstream of his thinking about religion. Religious ritual is a symbolic system, but rules of uncleanness lie outside this system. The main reason for this is that they often appear to be irrational. Arguing that 'uncleanness or dirt is that which must not be included if a pattern is to be maintained', Dr Douglas shows how seemingly irrational and arbitrary 'hygienic' ritual behaviour becomes meaningful once its own particular symbolism is understood. 'Pollution' symbolism relates to precisely the same reality as does 'holiness' symbolism. Whereas the latter demonstrates what must be included in the self-understanding of a particular society, the former makes a statement about what must be excluded if that self-understanding is to be preserved. Both kinds of symbol belong together in the same ritual language.

To illustrate her thesis, Dr Douglas turns to the Old Testament; in particular to the 'abominations of Leviticus'. (Lev. Ch. 11.) She proceeds to demonstrate that, once it is understood that for the Jew 'holiness is exemplified by completeness', it becomes clear also that for him the underlying principle of cleanness in animals is that they shall conform fully to their class; for only in this way can the general scheme of the world, that underlying order which is the expression of God's holiness, his perfection, be proclaimed. 'To be holy is to be whole, to be one: holiness is unity, integrity, perfection of the individual and of the kind.'[23]

This, of course, makes nonsense of Frazer's evolutionary scheme, which postulates the existence of irrational 'magical' rituals which have nothing at all to do with religion, 'sui generis'. Religion is primarily concerned with spiritual belonging and the preservation of an ideal of completeness, the struggle to attain to a perfect order, to shape a society which will share in divinity by making itself a mirror of divine perfection.

Indeed, we have reason to believe that the whole 'holiness–taboo–pollution' syndrome has more to do with considerations of meaning than with any purely practical concerns of safety and hygiene. Dr Douglas draws attention to the primary nature of religious belief in taboo-formation; and, as we have seen in Chapter 1, Levi-Strauss maintains that taboos do not emerge, or are not contrived, from ideas about self-preservation by the simple manipulation of the natural environment of the race, but from an aspiration towards the celebration of an ideal perfection, and the reproduction of that perfection within the social order; that is, from considerations of a wished-for wholeness, which gives its own meaning to a diversity of details. By concentrating upon the functional necessity or rationale of particular details within the system of taboo, and thence trying to induce the system from its parts, anthropologists have allowed the overall meaning to escape them; or rather, they have purposefully blinded themselves to the possibility of an overall meaning of a genuinely religious nature, a self-transcending meaning, whose whole is greater than the sum of its parts. By too intense study of the kind of trees, they have missed the vital shape of the wood.

Jewish taboos emerge from ideas about the meaning of the universe itself. They relate to, and constitute, a kind of grammar of belief, a language for the ordering of a certain quality of experience, God-experience. God has laid down certain rules for men. These rules are his own, in that they mirror his own perfections. Things which do not fit the divine scheme for human reality, animals which do not appear to conform as to physical characteristics or way of life to the divinely appointed 'norm', are called taboo, and are shunned.

9. However, we may still doubt whether the religion of Leviticus and Deuteronomy, even if it cannot be called 'irrational' and 'magical', would be held by Frazer to be authentically religious. It is not, after all, primarily concerned with ethical categories, in the abstract, or with making personal decisions, but with conformity to prescribed rules of social behaviour, as Mary Douglas says.

For Frazer, ethics are the hall-mark of mature religion, and any religion which is not rooted in an ethical understanding as such is bound to be 'primitive' and the mark of a civilisation which is not yet fully developed. It would not be strictly true to say that this idea is an invention of Frazer himself, although his anthropological doctrine has done much to establish it, for it represents a long established tradition in religious thought, the distrust of exterior religious enactments, and the exaltation of interior thought, feeling, attitude, intention. This is the posi-

tion, that of traditional Protestantism, from which Frazer begins his examination of the cultures of other races. The argument is a simple one: races are 'primitive' if their religion is
'primitive'; and their religion is primitive if it is not demonstrably ethical.

In fact, of course, the contrast between interior will and
exterior enactment, goes deep into the history of Judaism and
Christianity. 'The rage of the Old Testament Prophets was continually renewed against empty external forms, paraded instead of humble and contrite hearts.' How could it be otherwise?
Such a tension must exist in any religion which involves a
personal relationship with divinity, and in which religious considerations are held to affect the daily life of society and govern
the actions of men. Such a state of affairs is bound to
necessitate an attitude towards God (or towards the gods),
which is personal and individual, and regards religion as
primarily a matter of commitment and genuine devotion to
worship.

But the condition of tension is not always critical; the honest
distrust of outward form on the part of men of good faith need
not amount to the rejection of the artificial, the 'man-made', as
without spiritual value or religious significance of any kind.
The attitude of 'either/or', either the things of men, or the
things of God, which characterises the Puritan rejection of
ritual, is not simply a repetition of the prophetic teaching about
the cultus, for the prophets did not attack the *use* of ritual in
the worship of God, but its *mis*use. Mary Douglas cites the
custom in Old Testament criticism of setting 'the prophetic'
over against 'the priestly' as a notable example of that 'sheer
anti-ritualistic prejudice, which supposes that there can be a
religion which is all interior, with no rules, no liturgy, no external signs of inward states'.[23][30]

---

[30] 'The history of the Israelites is always presented as a struggle between
the prophets, who demanded interior union with God, and the people,
continually liable to slide back into primitive magicality.' *Purity and Danger*,
p. 25.

10. To press this argument further, the Old Testament is very commonly supposed to contain two opposing kinds of religion, a 'good' kind which is ethical, and a 'bad' kind which is magical and materialistic. The first kind is the forerunner of Christianity and represents progress and social enlightenment; the second kind represents the special customs and organisation of those neighbouring races whose influence the people of God were in the process of throwing off in their journeying towards the Kingdom. The prophets speak for the former, the priests and the cultus for the latter. But how much truth is there, in fact, in this judgement? First of all, is it in fact true that the prophets reject the cultus because it is ritualistic?

To the eighth-century prophets, the temple sacrifice was associated with a refusal to acknowledge the truth about God and his dealings with men. Chapter 5 of the Book of Amos maintains that religious festivals with music and burnt offerings are offensive to God if they take the place of right behaviour. 'I hate, I despise your feasts, and I take no delight in your solemn assemblies. Take away from me the noise of your songs: but let justice roll down like waters and righteousness like an overflowing stream.' (Amos 5: 21–24.) The prophets point out that the cultus may be, and in fact is being, used in the attempt to influence God and to persuade him to approve the actions of men, in contradiction of the insights of the Spirit concerning his nature and requirements. 'I desire loving-kindness, not sacrifice,' says Yahweh in Hosea 6: 6, 'the know-ledge of God rather than burnt offerings'. In this way ritual provides men with a means of escape from the responsibility of a real meeting with divinity; it is therefore an impious attempt to avoid the issue with regard to the known requirements of Yahweh.

However, what the prophets are attacking is not the cultus itself, but its patent corruption in their own time. They stress the need for reform rather than revolution. They certainly do not advocate the cultus's abolition, but its re-invigoration and renewal. In Pfeiffer's[34] words they 'moralized religion, but did not substitute morality for religion'.[31] Similarly, in *The Faith of Israel*, H. H. Rowley[35] warns against 'any simple antithesis between prophetic religion and the religion of the temple ... still more should we beware of suggesting that prophetic religion could dispense with the element of worship – not seldom the prophets are presented as men who were opposed to the entire worship of the temple, and who taught that God wanted only obedience in daily life'.[32]

11. Such warnings are certainly necessary. In *Prophecy and the Prophets*, T. H. Robinson maintains roundly that Amos, Hosea, Jeremiah, and Isaiah 'strenuously denounced ritual' and 'had no use for the sacrifice of the temple as a form of religion'.[33] I. G. Matthews, in *The Religious Pilgrimage of Israel* claims that the eighth-century prophets made social ethics 'the essential, even the sole requirements'[34] of worship. Indeed Pfeiffer himself, in *Religion in the Old Testament*, blames the prophets' toleration of ritual forms for 'the obliteration of the sharp line of demarcation drawn by Amos between the moral and the ceremonial'.[35] In *The Books of the Old Testament* (a work quoted by Dr Douglas) he says of the lawyer priests of the post-exile period that they 'sanctified the external, obliterated from religion the ethical ideals of Amos and the tender emotions of

[31] 'Their attitude resembles that of Jesus, who regarded prayer offered in a spirit of complacency as offensive to God, but who never advocated the abolition of prayer,' Vde Luke 18 : 10–14.
[32] In *Rite and Man*,[6] Bouyer says that 'Protestant Biblical exegesis, which was still handicapped by the unquestioned acceptance of Hegelian dialectics, had accepted as an axiom an essential opposition between prophet and priest, that is to say, between the man of the word, individually inspired by God, as he was thought to be, and the man of the rite and religious institutions.' This, however, 'was before it was established that the divine word, in all living religions, and particularly in those of the Mediterranean basin, is not only incorporated with ritual, but is essentially one with it'. In this connection he cites the work of Sigmund Mowinckel and S. H. Hooke.
[33] T. H. Robinson, *Prophecy and the Prophets*, 1923, pp. 190, 194.
[34] I. G. Matthews, *The Religious Pilgrimage of Israel*, 1947, p. 128.
[35] R. H. Pfeiffer, *Religion in the Old Testament*, p. 144.

Hosea, and reduced the universal creator to the status of an inflexible despot'.[36]

However the clinching argument concerns the central message of the Old Testament about the relationship between man and God. Professor Eichrodt totally rejects what he calls 'modern man's sentimental disparagement of the cultus', as running entirely counter to the distinctive religious understanding of Israel. This involved 'the subjugation of the entire national life to the Covenant with Yahweh'.[37] In this subjugation the cultus played the central role; for the Covenant relationship is a personal relationship; the cultus serves and expresses the Covenant between persons. Rites are capable of degenerating into an attempt to manipulate God, but they are never evolved in order to do so. The Covenant relationship is a gracious relationship, instituted by, and ultimately dependent on, God alone. The cultus is never conceived of as a way of influencing Yahweh. The crude notion that Yahwistic sacrifice benefits God in the sense of bribing Him with the flesh of animals implies an understanding of man's relationship with God which runs counter to all Old Testament teaching. God does not need to receive, *but man must give*.[38] The cultus provides men with an opportunity to express their responsiveness to God in a symbolic way, that is, as direct communication, by a concrete expression of feeling. The cultus is thus God's gift to men, and not their own invention – it is His provision for humanity, and in it, He keeps trust with His people. This idea is as much a part of the Old Testament as of the New.[39]

Protestant Old Testament commentators do not seem able to allow ritual anything but a grudging acceptance on the part of

[36] R. H. Pfeiffer, quoted in *Purity and Danger*, p. 62, 'he presents the religious history of Israel as if the stern, insensitive law givers were in conflict with the prophets, and never allows that both could have been engaged in the same service, or that ritual and codification could have something to do with spirituality'.

[37] *The Theology of the Old Testament*, S.C.M. Eichrodt, p. 92.

[38] 'The whole tenor of ancient Israel's belief in Yahweh is irreconcilable with the idea that God is fed by sacrifice, bound up as this is with God's dependence on man.' Eichrodt, op. cit., p. 92.

[39] Vde Luke 22: 10, I Corinthians 11: 24.

'prophetic religion'. And yet, as Eichrodt points out, the rite is the essential expression of a nation's corporate faithfulness; no community can worship together, as a community, without a framework of ritual. In Mary Douglas's words, 'as with society, so with religion, external form is the condition of its existence'. Where is the Protestant sect which does not have its specific rules of behaviour, its articles of belief, its particular mode of conducting a service? If it is to remain true to the teachings of its Lord, Christianity cannot avoid being a social religion: as such it is bound to abide by the rules which govern social reality and its particular modes of communication. However, the impression given by some writers is that such ritual worship is forced upon men by their lower natures, and that God would rather be worshipped in solitary privacy, as it were in a kind of ideal 'spiritual' vacuum. As we have seen, even when they are aware of its temptations, Protestant commentators seem unable to free themselves of this Manichean prejudice, which seems to be part and parcel of the Reformation attitude; but one feels that the Hebrew prophets were much more kindly disposed to ritual acts than are their Calvinistic successors.

The great prophets were accustomed after all, to externalising their spiritual understanding and insights in symbolic actions. Pfeiffer is no doubt right that they were 'puritans and individualists, participating in no corporate activity whatsoever', but their mission was to the nation at large. They functioned within a shared cultural inheritance, talking of religious matters in the language of the cultus, employing techniques for the mythical embodiment of religious truth with which their audiences were already familiar because of a shared background of temple religion. It is within the temple that Isaiah receives his commission, and from the temple that he emerges to witness to God among the people; it was within the temple that Jeremiah wore his wooden yoke[40]; and, indeed all his acted signs and those of other prophets are an endorsement of ritual

[40] Jer. Ch. 27, 28.

as a valid means for the communication of religious insights to other people, and of sharing religious experience with other people. To defend ritual is not to condone its misuse. Ritual can be the pledge and sign of a relationship which excludes the very possibility of magic and manipulation, a relationship of loving gratitude and deep loyalty. The greater the good, the greater the possibility of evil, where the good is perverted and all claim to a truly personal relationship with God denied. Ritual itself is merely a tool, to be used either for good ends or evil ones; but it is an essential tool, for social relations depend, as Mary Douglas points out, on symbolic acts. The tenor of prophetic utterance is always simply this, that a relationship must be held to precede its outward signs and symbols. The Prophets castigate emptiness and venality, and quite rightly. Once the relationship has been broken, no rite can restore it. The rite is the expression of a spiritual fact, not any kind of substitute for that fact.

There seems to be little evidence, then that the great prophets objected to ritual itself rather than to its employment in the service of teachings which they held to be erroneous. In fact, according to the religious understanding of the Jews, prophet and priest belong together: 'the same importance is given to moral and cultic transgressions' (Eichrodt). The cult is the expression of moral obedience and the people's desire for righteousness. There is no doubt that the kind of teaching favoured by the prophets set more store by right behaviour in everyday life than correct procedure in the sanctuary, and that Jews and Christians must endorse this attitude if they are to remain true to biblical revelation. But this is not to say that religions which employ ritual are necessarily less authentically spiritual than those which avoid ritual forms; indeed the work of some writers in the anthropology of religion would lead us to say exactly the opposite.[41]

[41] Dr Douglas, writing in *New Blackfriars* for June 1968, maintains that 'religious meaning is richer, and personal commitment deeper, in a ritualistic system than in one which shuns ritual'.

The Language of the Rite

13. We have seen that since Durkheim, some anthropologists have hesitated to regard religious ritual as magical, and have investigated its *expressive* rather than its *instrumental* function. We have maintained that the idea of magic is connected with the idea of the unexplained and the mysterious, that which 'lies outside the system'. However, it must be admitted that Durkheim's distinction between symbolic, or shared, ritual, and magical, or private ritual, which always remains secret and obscure, would not convince a follower of Frazer, who would maintain that both were magical, because both, the secret and the 'explained', are attempts to change reality in an 'unscientific' way. And since 'unscientific' is held to mean 'pre-scientific', both are 'primitive', used as a term of abuse or denigration. If the first sign of 'primitiveness' is acceptance of the non-rational, then the second is a preference for corporate ritual to personal ethics as a ratification of behavioural norms.

But the whole idea of 'the primitive' as it is applied to nations and societies which possess a different social organisation from our own has come under fire during the last half century, particularly in the work of Evans-Pritchard on the Nuer peoples, and Godfrey Lienhardt,[37] writing about the Dinka. These writers follow Durkheim in refusing to equate ritual with magic. Ritual is presented 'not as a mask over the face of living experience, but as that which creates and inspires it'. Lienhardt points out that, among the Dinka, ritual is valued as a way of communicating with divinity and with each other. It does not take the place of action in the world, but strengthens resolution with regard to such action: it is highly ethical, and results in a heightened and developed social consciousness. If this is magic, then religion itself is 'magical' and 'primitive', because it is concerned with relationships within a metaphysical community, a kind of social belonging that includes both men and God, and with the claims made by relationship, some of which do have the effect of altering reality – but by agreement, by a covenant of loyalty and love, not by force and manipulation. Sacramental forms and ritual actions simply establish and express this community. Dr Douglas equates ritualism in worship with a tightly knit community, and a well defined social group which is felt to be a source of comfort, support, encouragement and challenge to the individual who 'belongs'. In a description of Navaho religion, which from being a network of socio-religious rituals, has become personalised and interior, Dr Douglas says that 'here is a fascinating model of the Protestant reformation'.[42] She points out that the effect of this absence of rituals is actually to reduce the awe in which divinity is held, and to make God more like the individual who worships him. A greater sense of the otherness of God proceeds from formal worship than from the internalised confrontation with divinity, which is considered to be the type of those religions which centre upon personal behaviour and the ethical responsibility of the individual. Man, says Dr Douglas, needs this sense of otherness, of differentiation, in order to realise his identity with his fellow men, his social identity. He is much more likely to behave as a responsible person if his religion binds him to the community in which he lives, and provides him with a definition of the particular social role he is called on to play, his expectations from his fellows and his duty towards them, than if the tendency of his religion is to concentrate on a single relationship of 'ultimate demand and final succour', in the presence of which all other relationships take on the nature of distractions (New Blackfriars.; June 1968).

14. To conclude, then. The preference for personal and internalised religion may be taken as a symptom of a societal breakdown which is gradually encroaching upon the Western world. The 'Global Village' remains an idea rather than a reality. Information, even intellectual awareness, is not enough; there must be *incorporation*, a ratified and experienced citizenship. In the meantime it becomes more and more difficult to achieve

[42] 'God' (according to the Israelite understanding) 'is not the personification of ethics, but one who abides in a loyalty manifested in the concrete relationships of community.' Eichrodt, op. cit., p. 249.

a genuine sense of community in today's fragmental society. The urban society of the West is evolving away from any real understanding of corporate belonging, at least so far as the local community is concerned. In these circumstances it is difficult to see how a force which contributes so powerfully to the internalisation of the ethics of social belonging can be held to be 'primitive' in any pejorative sense of that word.

3 Rite and Time
(The Rite as Present Being)

1. The Ritual Symbol

We have discovered that ritual makes most sense if it is regarded as a language, a code of communication. But it is a
specialised kind of language, communicating a special kind of
knowledge. This knowledge is experiential, and it is knowledge
about three things: time, place, and relationship. These three
cannot really be separated within the ritual experience; indeed it might be said that their inseparableness and inter-
relation is what ritual is really about. Images of time, place, and
relationship are interchangeable in corporate rituals. Such images as the belly of a monster, the womb which is also, and at
the same time, a tomb, the tree which connects earth and
heaven, time and eternity, the paradise at time's beginning and
end, the clashing rocks or place of special danger which the
traveller must pass through on his journey towards a higher
plane of existence, are both temporal and spatial; and because
they are concerned with a reaching out across barriers towards
the unknown, they are also images of relation.

These images are true symbols; which is what we mean when

we say that the knowledge they communicate is experiential knowledge. It is a kind of 'three-dimensional' knowing. The symbol gives time the depth of spatial location, and space the significance of historical or supra-historical truthfulness. In a sense, the symbol *includes* space and time within itself and exerts a transforming, even a subjugating power over them, so that the present moment becomes all time and the place of revelation is a type of everywhere.

The symbol has the effect of synchronising past and future, the experience as it approaches us, and to which we reach out in eagerness, and our understanding and appreciation of that experience, its incorporation within the ranks of our other experiences.

Experiential knowledge – that which cannot be thought, but must, nevertheless, somehow be lived, and so lived *through*. Basically, the rite is a kind of substitute for simple thinking, the ordering and registration of reasons and events by the normal process of intellect. As such it presents itself as the proper tool for dealing with crisis situations. This is not to suggest that a person ought not to try to think rationally in the face of crisis, but that certain events in life are, or appear to be, so crucially important, so stunning in their impact, as to have a deadening effect upon the intellect's role as a mediator of experience to the self; instead, the intellect assumes the responsibility of defending the psyche against the violent shock of this new knowledge, so that the facts are 'rationalised away' instead of being translated by the event itself into a genuine experience, acting and re-acting within the real life of the person concerned.

Each crisis in our life has its appropriate and time-honoured ritual. What seems to be a defence against experience, a mere game played in order to distract us from reality, is a way into reality's very heart. To by-pass the 'frontal attack' of intellect is not, in the circumstances of traumatic shock, to avoid the truth – for years of training in moderating the shocks and buffets of life have rendered the conscious mind an untrustworthy mentor in the treatment of conditions which, although both painful and wounding to the present being of the self, may be, if properly faced and assimilated, potentially both healthful and even enriching.

And so we return to what is perhaps the principal function of the rite, that of allowing intellectually 'impossible' things to happen. What cannot, dare not, be thought, is somehow acted. Fear is the reason for ritual. But somehow the rite contrives to take fear into itself and make it work for truth, and, eventually, for acceptance. Relationship – love – is the only answer to fear; but in certain circumstances, particularly those involving some kind of critical confrontation, relationship seems impossible, either for intellectual reasons (reasons concerned with absurdity or illogicality), or for emotional ones (that is, reasons of guilt). But it still happens within the rite.

For the rite is the language of the un-thinkable. It is a way of 'living those things which do not bear thinking'. As such it is a necessary means of expression, for what cannot be thought must still, if it exists, be adequately taken into account, adequately recognised, for truth's sake. The fearful must be registered if the truth is to be lived. However the fact remains that it is considerably easier to *depict* a painful truth than to *contemplate* the same truth. Children who weep when they hear about the gingerbread man's fate, or tremble with sympathetic terror at the peril of Red Riding Hood, cheerfully act the same stories out, and learn from the experience. It is as though by standing back from an experience and contemplating it we allow anxiety to creep in between the event and ourselves. This is the anxiety of contingency, and also of responsibility; the anxiety which asks: 'What should I do if . . .?' By participation we gain a certain immediate release in acting.[1] In the rite we act *together*. We face the future together, and our guilt, our sense of limitation and uncertainty, is shared.

[1] 'Few love to hear the sins they love to act' – Pericles. Perhaps this is what Artaud means when he says that 'the image of a crime is infinitely more terrible than the same crime when actually committed'. But this does not apply to the temerity of the obviously culpable – it surely relates to a general 'lack of boldness in approaching the throne of grace'.

Symbolic ritual is a structure for *presenting* – making past and future, near and far, fact and fantasy, *present*. But this kind of experience, this kind of knowing is different from other kinds of knowledge. We are familiar with it in the theatre as well as in church. It owes its quality of presentness to its immediacy. Whatever is immediate is present. Time, with its power to modify and limit, its power to *reduce*, has been banished. The symbol is not about meaning and value recognised as ultimate or triumphant; it *is* that meaning and that value as it may be known in its fullness, sending its roots deeper into the human soul than any one-sided appeal to the intellect could do. Within the symbol, past, present, and future may be juxtaposed as in a play, so that all is made to serve the meaning which inspires and precedes it;[2] indeed meaning itself is all that reaches us. We become aware of an ideal truth, a truth which has been stripped of its time-scale, and with it of its contingent and particularised nature, and provided with a structure for happening here and now, and for including us in the immediate experience of things which demand, not our detached contemplation or our rational assessment, but our surrender and our participation.

The symbol itself is impersonal, yet it communicates personality; in itself it defies all time-limits, it is 'the still centre of the turning world', and yet it makes use of action within time; its significance is cosmic or extra-cosmic, yet it addresses itself to individuals, establishing them in the integrity of personality. The myth, the exemplary life of the hero or heroes, and the rite in which this is re-enacted and re-lived, meet only in the symbol. Transcendence and immanence touch at this point only. The rite is not bound to the myth, in the sense of being congruent with it. Both myth and rite pivot on the symbol, which draws meaning, power, and life from the former and

[2] This, surely is the purpose and the effect of the cinematographic 'flashback'. We may note also the use of the 'present historic' in the telling of stories. Children frequently use the present tense when they are recounting past adventures, in order to get the point over with the greatest possible vividness.

uses it to enrich the latter's own existence and innate life, even as the myth gains immediacy and power from the real presence of the men and women taking part in the rite. The exemplary life provides the myth; its significance for the present life of mankind provides the symbol; the symbol becomes translated into common experience as it is 'acted out' within the rite. In other words, the life of the hero is the myth, the myth's significance is the symbol, the symbol's embodiment is the rite. We might say that the movement of the rite is 'from flesh to flesh via the symbol'.

Religious symbols are the lingua-franca of the religious consciousness, a fact which explains the recurrence of identical symbolism in religions which are philosophically and theologically entirely dissimilar.[3] So long as religion means idealism and aspiration it will employ symbols of death and re-birth, pilgrimage, peril, and paradise. The religious mechanism of the rite lends itself to the particular understanding about the relationship between humanity and divinity which we call the myth. The truth of any particular religion must depend on its own understanding of the nature of that relationship; its particular and distinctive claim on our acceptance, its ability to relate historical events and eternal truths, its revelatory power with regard to life in this world in the face of the generalising effect of an universal morphology of rituals.

2. *Pre-liminal Rituals: The Doorway into the Present*

The basic message of the rite is this: that real life in time, real humanity, is only attainable by means of eternity. The present

---

[3] Jung has made us familiar with the idea that religious symbolism in general makes use of images of an ideal truth taking archetypal form in the collective unconscious of mankind. With regard to the Christian faith we might note the opinion of two writers, the first a Roman Catholic, the second a Calvinist. In *Symbols of Christ*, Damasus Winzen[2] says that 'many signs of the Messias have a cosmic character. The tree, the mountain, the Sun, the Cornerstone, the Star in the Old Testament, the Pearl, the Grain of Wheat, the Fountain, the Door, the Lamp, the Fish in the New Testament, are all deeply rooted in the common spiritual experience of mankind.' And Karl Barth says, 'the finality of the Christian religion can only be apprehended by faith', and not by the uniqueness of its mode of expression.

only becomes itself when it comes into contact with (in ritual terms, when it is homologised with) the eternal. The way in which this is brought about in religious rituals is dramatically explicit. The past is killed and the present incorporated with eternity. Thus, in surrendering to the mechanism of the rite the participant finds himself driven onwards; he has no option but to move forwards into the future, for his exit is cut off by his own symbolic death and the death of the hero-figure with whom the rite identifies him and with whom he identifies himself.

A repeated pattern in religious ritual involves two deaths. In the course of his encounter with a ferocious monster which has oppressed and terrified the whole race, the hero is himself killed, or at least suffers terrible hardships. However, he survives his ordeal and manages to slaughter his oppressor, emerging from the monster's belly, from the very jaws of death, to wreak a terrible revenge. This scenario is re-enacted by those taking part in the rite, who are, ritually 'killed' and 'restored', thus participating in the hero's victory. Such rites may signify that the participants have embarked upon a new level of socio-religious belonging within society as a whole, or that they have been received into an autonomous secret society, or chosen to perform some specific religious duty in the community as priest or shaman; or they may be repeated by members of a religion as a means of corporate and personal renewal and re-direction.[3]

We might say that, within the symbolism of Christian ritual, the monster-figure represents death itself; but he is universally the presence that must be shunned, must be done away with, if the transcendant purpose of the rite is to be achieved. He is, in fact, all that holds, or has held, the race or the individual back; he is sin, shortcoming, limitation, the hostile environment; he is the past that must be surpassed. He is always, therefore, a kind of death, so far as death is the negation of on-going life and purpose and growth. Thus the message of the rite is that the past can only be transcended at great cost; for not only the past, but *our own part in the past*, must perish – *we* must perish, *we* must be killed, in order to begin again. We 'rise to higher things over the stepping stones of our dead selves'. We can survive only if our own experience is homologised to that of the exemplary hero, the 'Original Survivor'. The action of reliving this revelatory scenario abolishes the temporality which we fear, over which we have no control – where meaning constantly eludes us while drawing us back into itself, swallowing up our aspirations and vitiating our idealism.

Thus the rite prepares and enables us for the future by disarming the past. Not all past time, but our own past in its negative aspect, the past which drains the present of its meaning and significance, of its life. The rite allows us to understand in the present and live in the present. At the same time it recalls and makes present that part of the past which allows the present to be itself, the moment when negativity was finally conquered and the monster killed. That part of the past, the saving history of the race, is always available, constantly realised in the rite. Thus the rite says 'now *is* the time' by saying 'then *was* the time'.

In this way ritual allows certain privileged events in the history of the race to irradiate and transform the whole of existence. Incidents in the past which lie outside the tradition of the saving events are ritually redeemed by association with them. The ritual action is redemptive *by association*. The past can now be re-stated and its ideal significance asserted. Ritual becomes, in Mary Douglas's words 'a visible expression of a well-formed wish'. The rite gives vigour and purpose to action and definition to experience; it allows men to step boldly into the future out of a present which is no longer haunted by the imperfections and failures of the past. Ritual ties up the loose ends of past experiences; it lays the past to rest, having extracted from it the life and power, the *idealised* life and power which it has to bequeath to the present, the significance that the present needs to be itself.

This, then, is the perfect time recalled by ritual, and not some vague eternity which is distinguishable from our 'ordinary' life in time mainly because of its mythical and 'idealistic' nature. This idealism is a revolutionary force of irresistible power. The 'dreaming time of the world's beginning' is recalled because of its transforming vitality, as the milieu of great events which when realised in the present, have the power to change an existential lack into a fullness and perfection of present being. Within the rite it is the intensity of the experience that suspends time, not any kind of escape from involvement in reality. The initiand faces reality to the extent of being swallowed up by his own truth, by the existential burden which presses so heavily upon him, the weight of all his thoughts, words and works, in other words, his responsibility for himself. Thus he surrenders to the past which he wishes to transcend in order to wrest from it a redeemed present and the hope of a final victory in the future.

This is the basic ritual dynamism, the source of the rite's power to change the quality of life. The death of the past gives the rite life, making it an eternal moment, a supreme value, yielding those who take part in it to Being as a present possibility. This dramatic scenario of death and resurrection belongs primarily to rituals which are explicitly religious, and which involve a sudden access of Spirit, enabling those involved in them to undertake great responsibilities and charismatic vocations. Initiation into secret societies and individual ordination ceremonies lay great stress upon the death and subsequent resurrection of initiands. They are more explicit historically, as well as being more violent than those rites of passage which at one stage of his life or another involve every member of a society. By means of personal suffering, the initiand enters into a condition of life homologous to that of a demiurgic god or hero. The truth to be learnt from the rite is more a truth about culture than about nature – in other words it is a historical or a mythological truth about the childhood of the race and the relationship between God and man through a mediator. But even here the result is beneficial to society as a whole, and not only to those who take part in it in order to achieve personal sanctity; for the rite incorporates the presence of sacred personages in a way which involves 'a complete regeneration of society and cosmos'.[3]

Such a renewal is the explicit purpose of rites which are directly social, such as those which accompany puberty; but even these have moments of terror and trauma for the young people concerned which are analogous to an experience of dying and being restored to life. Indeed, puberty rites, rituals of initiation into secret societies, ceremonies of ordination to shamanistic or priestly office, all follow the same basic pattern, which is capable of reduction in scale and intensity, so that even the most trivial corporate ceremony involves some kind of dying to an old state of affairs and embracing a new one, some kind of movement into and out of a moment of change; and even in the most commonplace and least stressful ceremony this moment of change possesses some intensity, some need to be formalised and accepted. In the significant corporate rituals of social belonging, or deep personal commitment, however, we see that this is what ritual is really *about*. Ritual is about change, and the terrors and uncertainties which surround change, but which must somehow be 'accepted into the system', both corporate and personal. It is about mankind's fear of novelty, of unstructured situations and states of flux, in which the old way is over and done away and the new has not yet really begun; it is about life without existential guide-lines, when man must launch himself out into the unknown; it is about the fear of the threshold, the need to plot new areas of experience and mark out the 'existential lebensraum'. Anthropologists point to a recurring preoccupation with social barriers, a neurosis of frontiers; psychologists remind us of the anxiety which inevitably accompanies times of challenge and crisis. These things are contained within the ritual moment. The rite is a mechanism for living through existential crises, for facing anxiety and coping with it in a way which is socially acceptable and personally honest. It is also a way of *sharing* anxiety at the point where the personal and the social meet, the point where the past must be superseded and the future faced with dignity and courage.

As Eliade[3] says, 'the process of initiation seems to be co-existent with any and every human condition'. Every human condition that is, contains the possibility that the change which it inevitably involves (for all life involves change), may be endorsed by a definite, willed, movement of the soul. In this way it may attain to be a real 'moment of truth'. Crystallised into the action of corporate ritual, it becomes a sign-post for existence, rooted in the acceptance of the past and pointing hopefully to the future. The rite, whether it be of immense social and personal significance or of relatively circumscribed scope and incidental importance, always asserts the autonomy of the present moment, its eligibility as opportunity for casting off preoccupations which belong to past time and for-mer states, its willingness ready and open to face the future. In its most dramatic form it is associated with ceremonials of entry into existential states which are radically different, with what van Gennep[5] calls pre-liminal rites, empowering us to seize hold of present being while signing the death warrant of our past existence.

3. *Liminal Rituals: A Pause in Time*

After the drama of the pre-liminal rite comes the period of stasis, the germination of new life. Initiation rites into secret societies resemble the corporate rites of passage which operate in whole cultures because the initiatory scenario is everywhere the indispensable symbol of a reaching after a more sacred way of being in the world. But where the sacredness which is sought after is one of a more complete union with nature, rather than a transformation of nature by divinity and its chosen instru-ments, the liminal stage of germination and preparation for the new birth assumes a greater importance than the moment of initiatory death, the time of decision and sacrifice.

These rites stress the notion of timelessness and of a return to the womb. The liminal period of the shamanic initiation may involve the total and salutory re-shaping of the individual's personality, in which he is, as it were, 'stripped down to the bare bones of his being'. He finds himself involved in a return to chaos, symbolic but very real. Thus he faces the terrors of formlessness in order to achieve new form. But in most puberty rites this middle period is a time of instruction and growth, and its symbolism is of generation and gestation rather than specifically of purgatory and the refinement of essences. This is the real 'time-out-of-time', in which a new generation of adult members of society is created. The symbol of the tomb, although still necessary because it implies a 'dying to the profane condition', presents its other face and appears now as the womb in which new life is forming. The experience of pre-liminal death is valued in such social rites because it allows the novices to benefit from the instruction of their tribal ancestors, or, rather, of those who are inspired to represent them. The experience of initiatory dying also provides a barrier against the immediate past which is exceedingly hard to penetrate. The life of childhood is finally and dramatically left behind. Those who rest in the corporate womb, in the rite's central area, are refreshed by contact with sacred, timeless, eternal things; and the contact is made outside time, in the special symbolic milieu of a ritual separation. In a sense this liminal period, which is the pivotal point at which life begins afresh, and images of death become images of life, is the real 'ritual time', the deeply ambiguous 'dreaming time', when the past is left behind and the future not yet begun. Again, it belongs to all corporate rituals, as it belongs to the action of growth, the movement of self-transcendence. But here, in the rite's centre, the growth is not yet visible; or rather it is non-linear, qualitative rather than quantitative, a suspension of potentiality within an actual stillness and repose. It is 'the still point of the turning world', and its holiness proceeds from the nominal intensity of feeling and significance which lives, paradoxically, at the rite's core of silence.

Here, ritual stands for undifferentiated Being, for the place where there is neither life nor death as we understand them, because there is no *existence*. Here we return in our own religious rituals for refreshment, light, and peace, coming back to the place without death for release from our natural fears; to the place of no life, in order to be born again into life. On the one hand we have the bliss of Eden, on the other the darkness of the tomb three days before Easter Sunday. This experience of no-experience is necessarily brief. We cannot stop permanently in either condition. We cannot install ourselves anywhere. We are simply passing through in the process of becoming. These 'times-out-of-time' help us to adjust to a new situation, a new stage in our development, to the reality of our developing and growing, and changing. Because they belong to the potent world of symbol, they not only register our progress but also constitute it; they participate in that to which they point.

The person who takes part in ritual is in a privileged position, in the sense that the disadvantage which he suffers in being temporarily cut off from the world allows him to concentrate in an unique way upon the world he has left behind and on its meaning and significance to himself. All his powers of feeling, perceiving, and understanding of himself and his environment are focused in an experience of heightened being. The ritual period of initiation is no mere hibernation; it is the lfe that he has left behind which appears as 'a sleep and a forgetting', not his present life. The candidate in an archaic initiation rite is subjected to life in a violent and concentrated form. Indeed, he or she may be made to suffer intensive physical and emotional pain, anxieties, conflicts, awakenings, deliverances. This ritual death is also a life, not only in theory but in acted fact; this distance is also an involvement, this holiness is also a profanity. In this privileged place at this special time, almost anything can happen.

4. *Post-liminal Rites: Time Renewed*

The completion of the rite brings with it a new mode of being. In some cultures and in some ritual scenarios we find a definite 'rite of emergence'. Many religions make provision for such a rite in, for example, their funeral rituals. A 'secondary burial' of a symbolic nature follows the liminal period of mourning. A gravestone is erected, ashes are scattered, a special memorial service is held (as distinct from a 'pre-liminal' service of commendation or committal, which has been held previously). The mourning rite is now over, and an event, as well as a person, is held to be properly laid to rest. Post-liminal rites, while they are part of any true ritual complex, are particularly suited to dealing with unfinished business. They mark the end of the old and the beginning of the new. They do not *allow* the old to come to an end; they are not powerful, not traumatic enough for that – but they lay it gently to rest and its attendant emotions with it, once it has died. They are ritual in function as a milestone rather than a revolution.

Psychologically of course, they play a key part in personal and social adjustment, because they express acceptance of the new reality and help us to identify with it. They say 'amen' to what has already come to pass. At their most hopeful and productive, post-liminal rites are the type of all rituals of acceptance and welcome. New life has begun and, in its vigour and certainty, it is able to accommodate all that is past within itself. This new life does not obliterate what went before; on the contrary it establishes it, giving it a retrospective completeness.

In a sense, all funeral rites are post-liminal, for they are a means of renewing time, starting it up again. In funeral ceremonial, the entire rite – the pre-liminal service (the funeral service proper), the ritualised wake or mourning period, and the post-liminal rite – partakes of the nature of the final service. In some cultures the final rite is actually a re-burial; in others the actual service of interment or cremation may follow the wake, and the pre-liminal rite be reduced to a short service of commendation of the soul of the departed and thanks-giving for his life.

Sometimes this is reduced to an absolute minimum. In the Irish wake-culture, for example, the main stress falls on the liminal and post-liminal rituals. The wake itself signifies a return to chaos, a release from the restraints of normal 'good behaviour' and propriety, a real cultural disintegration, analogous to the dissolution of the deceased's earthly identity and authority. The final requiem and burial are thus islanded in time, and attain a kind of post-cathartic solemnity, the deliberation of grief acknowledged and accepted, the calm of all passion spent. Such post-liminal rites act as monuments to whatever has gone before; not only the death of people or animals,[4] but of institutions, epochs, stages of growth, even attitudes of mind. They are real 'rites of passage'.

In a sense the 'return to Eden' is always a death, in that it constitutes a radical departure from existence in order to prepare for a genuine new birth. Eliade[3] describes how, in archaic societies, man's fear of dying is considerably eased, and his thinking about his latter end considerably affected, by an acceptance of the role of death as the indispensable precondition of any new life, the concommittant of all change, development, and growth. Death is the means of all entry into the spirit, and Spirit is life, so that 'death is the supreme means to spiritual regeneration ... the men of archaic societies strove to conquer death by according it such importance that death ceased to present itself as a cessation, and became a Rite of Passage'. There is simply no progress, no future, without a dying. The dissociation of the new from the old must be brought home in the most positive and striking way; the past is not merely allowed to fade away; all that belonged to the former condi-

---

[4] The death of animals and birds, particularly of domestic pets and garden creatures, provides a good example of the post-liminal role of funerary rituals. It is surprising how a short prayer and the interment of the dead sparrow, rabbit, guinea pig, or whatever, in a cardboard box, will satisfy a grieving child, and put an end to floods of tears which seemed unstoppable.

tion must be immolated in order to achieve a separation which is real. In such societies 'even violent death is creative in the sense that the life which is sacrificed manifests itself in a more brilliant form upon another plane of existence'. As 'the first condition of all mystical regeneration', the presence of death is symbolised in some way or another in all those rituals which are intended to mark the attainment of a recognised stage in human development – birth, puberty, marriage, widowhood, etc. So much is everywhere apparent: 'death followed by resurrection – the theme common to all initiations'.[3]

It is important to stress, however, that such symbolic deaths are almost always regarded as beneficial, in that they mark a return to goodness. The Being to which we return is in every way preferable to the alienated world in which we are accustomed to pass our lives. The course of our own individual development runs alongside the course of the world through time, so that, to revisit the time and place of the world's making is to enjoy the benefits of a new creation within ourselves. Such, at any rate, is the conscious or unconscious assumption of those who take part in such rituals. The fact that nature can be seen to fit so very easily into a human context is evidence of people much less alienated, much more at peace than we are ourselves. Unfortunately this tends to be true even if we are Christians, and subscribe to a theology of everlasting life, life emerging from death. Somehow our theology does not come home to us as powerfully as it should.

We begin now to see the necessity for the language of ritual. Ritual is able to say things that cannot be said in any other language. These things are, apart from the ritual experience, experiential nonsense: that, for instance, existence can somehow 'catch up' with, and run parallel with, being itself; and logical absurdity: that time can actually be interfered with and stopped. And it says them convincingly, unforgettably even. In Eliade's words, the rite is the expression of 'a strong and essentially religious desire to transcend an apparently irreducible existential situation and attain a total mode of being'. The rite is the way we talk of temporal and spatial impossibilities, and by giving them expression according to its form, incorporate them into our world of meaning. The rite is the language of embodied aspiration which becomes fact on becoming translated into ritual action.

5. *Modern Man and Time*

Rituals then, are a way of putting time to work in order to make the very best use of it. They are a way of 'improving' time, rendering it fuller, richer, deeper, more flexible, more *liveable*. They are concerned with the difficulties of life in time, difficulties of which modern man is very much aware. Indeed, we might say that modern Western man has a very definite 'time problem'. If religious rituals can help him with this problem, their relevance is obvious.

Western culture since the time of the Renaissance has been primarily concerned with the senses. That is to say, it has concerned itself with the material values of this world – wealth, influence, physical comfort. Such an attitude provides a favourable climate for the application of Freudian approaches to anthropology and for the development of physical science, but it leaves untouched deep cravings of the human spirit which imperiously demand satisfaction. It is apparent to theologians, philosophers, psychotherapists, alike that man needs some deep and worthwhile meaning in his life, some transcending value to which he can dedicate himself, even in which he may be said to lose himself. In grasping for this meaning, this purpose of life, man bursts the bonds of his conditioning factors and fashions his own future. The very search for meaning is the expression of his freedom, for 'even the fact that man is a part of nature, arises from nature, exerts great control over it, but ultimately is defeated by nature, nevertheless testifies to his transcendence, for he *knows* that this is his relationship to nature'.[6]

The awareness of freedom and autonomy, the awareness of transcendence, of an existential *separation* from the world, is the locus of man's search for his own meaning; it is in fact the terms of the problem of meaning. In a world where man and his environment simply explain each other there is no such problem. But modern attempts to construct a 'viable public universe' seem no more satisfactory to the man who seeks to find himself *as* himself, that is through the exercise of his own freedom, than were the now discarded attempts of previous ages. One by one, the various systems have collapsed over the centuries like so many great Medieval castles; Aristotle's cosmological fortress before the besieging army of advancing scientific understanding which followed the Copernican revolution; Aquinas's theological one before the upsurge of Reformation nonconformity and the Calvinistic proclamation of the 'impossibility' of God's demand. In its Marxist form the 'logo-logical' system, as Buber calls it, of Hegel still holds its own; but many would agree with Buber that such a system involves 'a reduction of humanity and the dispossessing of the human person and community in favour of universal reason, its dialectical processes and objective structures'.[7]

Typically, modern Western man regards himself very much as a special case. He is encouraged to do so by the novels he reads, by generations of plays, paintings and poems which emphasise the uniqueness of the individual human personality. He makes his own terms with the world, with other people, with God. He has 'come of age'. He expresses himself as himself. He resists explanation in accordance with scientific theory or religious doctrine. *He* will do the explaining, as the condition of his freedom. His freedom is more valuable to him than anything else in the world. 'I may give myself of my own free will – but I am not to be taken, sub-sumed, categorised, included. At least not in any real or fundamental sense. Fundamentally, I am free.'

Freedom is possibility; but it is also anxiety.[8] The problem may be stated thus: We see that in order to be free, man has to distance himself from the world. In order to find a meaning for his separate personal existence, he must take into account the fact of his separation from the world which presents itself to him as the source of all publicly verifiable meaning. Meaning is sacrificed to freedom; to be free at a distance from the world causes him deep pain. He knows that essentially he belongs to the world and has his being in the world. Somehow, then, he has to discover a way of giving himself to the world. Only in the courageous exercise of his freedom will he find himself.

To put this in another way; man is handicapped in his attempts at *being* by his obsession with *having*. He wants to have security, satisfaction, autonomy; and he wants to have them without involvement, merely to amass experiences of things and of people as a background to his experience of himself, to give himself reality and depth. In fact the process has the reverse effect, so that he loses the sense of his own being, his own bodily presence in the world of tangible objects. Being, it seems, cannot be so secured. Being is not something one gets, something one *has*. Having and Being may not be distinguished in this way at all. 'In order to *have* effectively,' says Gabriel Marcel, 'it is necessary to *be* in some degree, that is to say, to be immediately for one's self, to feel one's self as it were affected or modified.... There is,' he says, 'a mutual interdependence of having and being.'[9] In other words, it is necessary for a man to be *involved in the world*, involved as a participant, and not merely as a collector of experiences. Modern schizoid man attempts to construct a sense of identity, instead of earning it.

Although by now something of a cliché, alienation is neither a fallacy nor an invention of psychologists and philosophers. It is a fact. We may say that it represents a fear of, or anxiety about, that distance between the self and the self's experiencing of itself which occurs whenever questions about being are raised internally by the self; it corresponds also to the separation between separate selves experienced 'transcendentally'. It is the rejection of diversity and heterogeneity by the self which strives to reduce all experience to the unity of undifferentiated Being, to an unbroken and unchallenged certainty of self-hood. Freudian and post-Freudian psychologists are accustomed to draw from the almost universal presence of this fear, certain conclusions about the primal state of the human organism within the maternal womb and during the first few weeks after the infant's birth. A philosopher such as Sartre, however, simply accepts it as given. The whole of *Being and Nothingness*[10] (and it is over 600 pages long) is taken up with the notion of human existence as quite simply a lack. We experience ourselves as a lack of being: our entire life revolves around the distance between the self as it is experienced and the self as it is in itself. I am nothing in search of my own being. Worse than this, I exist by *intending* to be nothing. I am separated from my being by a nothingness for which I am myself responsible. In order to differentiate myself from Being-Itself and so find myself in freedom, I perpetually distance myself from being so that I may be my own being.

Mankind, in fact, is the being who has to be his own being. To put this another way: Sartre defines the essence of man as his freedom. Through choosing, Sartre argues, each individual creates both himself and his world, 'for human reality to be is to choose one's self'. Man is a nothingness over against a being which he never experiences as himself, simply because it *need not be* himself. Hence his intolerable anxiety.[5]

Living in this distance between consciousness of consciousness, which is freedom without security, and consciousness of being, which is security without freedom, it is no wonder that man is 'anxious'. This continual self-alienation is internal – i.e. the distance which separates self from being (or, as Sartre puts it, the 'for-itself' from the 'in-itself') is actually a product of the self

[5] 'If I may use a down-to-earth image for the sake of making my thought clearer, picture an ass drawing behind him a cart. He attempts to get hold of a carrot which has been fastened at the end of a stick which in turn has been tied to the shaft of his cart. Every effort on the part of the ass to seize the carrot results in advancing the whole apparatus and the cart itself which always remains at the same distance from the ass ... We run towards ourselves, and we are, due to this very fact, the being which cannot be reunited with itself.' *Being and Nothingness*, p. 122.

in its effort to be *itself*.[6] Sartre holds man directly responsible for his own negativity. He is the inventor of negation, the sole repository of nothingness. 'For himself' he is nothing in search of something. We shall return later to this idea of Sartre's.

Thus, according to the Existentialist writers of this century, the primary cause of mankind's anxiety is just this; an overriding concern with the problem of being. Man is anxious how to Be. He has either lost the ability (Marcel,[9] Camus,[12] Tillich), or he has never had it (Sartre[10]). His loss is signified to him by a divided consciousness; or, rather, by the knowledge of a separation between his existence, or his 'life', which is

---

[6] This is not an 'exterior' distance, in the sense that it is not pre-existent. Being alone is; there is no corresponding cosmic category or power of 'non-being', by which being is threatened, as in Heidegger and Tillich, 'Human reality is its own surpassing toward what it lacks; it surpasses itself toward the particular being which it would be if it were what it is. Human reality is not something which exists first in order to lack this or that; it exists first as lack, and in *immediate* synthetic connection with what it lacks' (p. 89); but human reality *can not be* what it *is* – 'the "pour-soi" is a being for whom his being is in question in his being, inasmuch as this being is a certain manner of not-being a being which he posits at the same stroke as other than he. Consciousness reveals the world in being not the world, and makes it that there is a world, but adds nothing to it.' (*Being and Nothingness*, p. 183.) Thus, where Heidegger holds that those experiences of nausea, worthlessness, absurdity which sometimes take us unawares are evidence of 'the impenetrable otherness of brute existence which subtends the construction of the intelligible world' and seeks always to destroy that world, and Tillich isolates a 'realm' of 'non-being' which is ontologically as basic as being, the stuff from which being was distinguished by the act of creation and the 'ontological condition of negative judgement' (*The Courage to Be*), Sartre holds man directly responsible for his own negativity. We may note that the presence of negation in man's universe is accounted for in psychoanalysis by the destructive instinct' ... 'some portion (of which) remains permanently within' the human psyche. (*An Outline of Psychoanalysis*[11]) This kind of thinking is entirely too concrete for the Existentialists, however. C.f. also Ian Suttie, *The Origins of Love and Hate*: 'Freud regards love and hate as wholly independent of each other in their own origin, as conflicting in "ambivalence", and as uniting in sadism and masochism. I do not take this view, but regard hate as the frustrated aspect of love, as "tails" is the obverse of "heads" in the same penny.' Suttie goes on, 'the whole story of the crucifixion (seems) to illustrate free forgiving, on the understanding that hate and evil have no independent existence, but are merely the frustration-forms of love itself, distorted as protest, reproach, and that kind of aggression which is originally intended to *compel* attention'.

somehow elusive and ambiguous, and Being-Itself, reality, solidity, absolute-ness, which is both tangible and quite unattainable. In Camus's phrase, man has 'an appetite for the absolute and for unity' which he cannot reconcile with the 'impossibility of reducing this world to a rational and reasonable principle'.[12] Camus advises him to accept the fact of this cosmic division between abstraction and worldly presence, and so to find a kind of liberty and a measure of release. Somehow he must escape from the torturing problem of abstraction which clings inseparably to a certain attitude of being in the world, an attitude of *mind* which, consciously or unconsciously, sets mind above all things, preferring it to all other *human* things. Man, says Camus, is not really free at all, for he is imprisoned by his own absurdity. But by accepting or even welcoming the absurdity of his search for 'being-through-understanding', he may attain freedom to 'be-as-absurd'. 'The hell of the present is his kingdom at last'; he will 'choose to look unflinchingly at a burning and frigid, transparent and limited universe, in which nothing is possible but everything is given ... to live without appeal in the passionate immediacy of his revolt against Being'. The keyword would seem to be 'immediacy'. The problem of being remains, but involvement with the world has somehow changed its nature. It is now something which can be lived *in* rather than *against*. It has become at once more intense and more bearable. Man's pain has been taken into the world which gives it birth, and so it attains a reality which is denied it in isolation. And it is *reality* which we seek. 'Crushing truths perish from being acknowledged. One must imagine Sisyphus happy.'[12]

By his 'sensibility of the absurd', which is also the truth about men, Camus gives himself to life-as-mystery. The same acceptance of mystery as a presence which bridges the gap between existence and being is to be found in Gabriel Marcel.[9] Like Camus, Marcel is determined to locate the problem inside this world. Being must be seen to be here and now. The idea of being must be made available to men as a blessing upon *this* life, *this* creation.[7] Thought creates a space between our-selves and being. Life, says Marcel, is experienced as having. We have experiences, ideas, material and spiritual possessions. All we know is what we have, not what we are. Existence itself is what we *have*; while being is what we *are*. But, he says, there is one vital exception to this, for we number among our other possessions a body. Our body is the vital link between what we have and what we are; for it is not simply a 'having'; it is also, unavoidably, a 'being'. A man's senses are witnesses to his own being. More than this – his bodily presence is a having which can participate in Being, can as it were leap the gap be-tween Being and having by simply *refusing to have*, by giving itself away and becoming 'disposable'. But he can only give himself away to others, he cannot make a gift to nothingness. Again, he cannot just opt out by committing suicide, for 'the being who is absolutely disposable for others does not allow himself the right to dispose freely of himself'.[9] Disposability, then, is the movement outwards from the self to the other across the chasm of thinking and distinguishing, which chasm is the symbol of our having. 'Love transcends the opposition of the same to the other by planting us in Being.'[9] Because I have a body, because I live in the world, I can give myself away as a real proposition. I have something to lose, and conse-quently something to gain. My body allows me to be by means of having, when I give what I have to another. The division between consciousness and its objects, between self and other and self and *itself*, regarded as objectifiable, that distance which seems to cut me off from the reality of Being, is not a problem to be reasoned, but the metaphysical truth which allows us to be in the first place. It is the way in which we find our true being in the mystery of relationship, in our real presence to other people and to the world. For the more I am present to

[7] 'My deepest and most unshakeable conviction – and if it is heretical, so much the worse for orthodoxy – is, that whatever all the thinkers and doctors have said, it is not God's will at all to be loved by us *against* creation, but rather glorified *through* the creation, and with the creation as our starting point.' *Being and Having*, p. 147.

another, the more I am present to myself, the greater my density, my realisation of self-hood, my plenitude of being. Thus, my body, which I *have*, enables my being, which I *am*, to share in the being of others. I am directly conscious of this sharing as an experience of Being-Itself.

These writers – Marcel, Camus, Sartre, along with many other twentieth-century witnesses – see man's search for meaning as a search for engagement. This may be an interior engagement, as Sartre 'flees the being without foundation which I was towards the founding act which I can be only in the mode of the would-be',[10] or an exterior one, as with Albert Camus, 'a world where everything is given and nothing explained'.[12] Or it may be both interior and exterior, as with Gabriel Marcel, who sees man as the slave of his own powers of disengagement both in himself and in the world he lives in. It is Marcel however, who shows us the way out of our dilemma. The revelation of the practical ability of the human corporal presence to bridge the gap between two worlds, the world of existence and the primary world of Being-Itself, leads Marcel towards a solution of the problem of mankind's alienation in terms of its expansion into the inclusive mystery of Being. But his solution is a religious one; his 'disposability', is in fact the Christian 'agape'. It is love as final value, love as the explanation of existence; as reconciliation and relationship; as that gift of Being to existence which transforms existence into Being in the crucial act of self-giving. Truth, says Marcel, can come only through the operation of love. In love, body and spirit, having and being, co-inhere. Love, in fact is having in order to give; and its symbol is the body. This is 'the essential ontological dictum'.[9]

The answer to the problem of dis-engagement then, is the experience of the mystery of unification. We find ourselves in the realm of the Ideal, of the Absolute, of God. The realm of that longed-for accession of Being, that 'fullness of life' in which all problems are resolved by being transcended. We see how near the truth Sartre is when he locates our disengagement *within ourselves* as an existential lack. 'The ideal fusion of the lacking with the one which lacks what is lacking is an unrealisable totality which haunts the for-itself and constitutes its very being as a nothingness of being.'[10] So says Sartre. In the mystery of religious faith, which is an exercise of self-giving in response to the self-giving of Being-Itself, this 'unrealisable totality' becomes a presence to men. It becomes at least intermittently realisable. It is intermittently realised. This is not to say that the religious person moves right out of the world of the problematic into the mystical world of one-ness with God as an unbroken experience; but it does mean that his consciousness of discontinuity and imperfection, his alienation from Being-Itself, is now seen within the context of an experience of unity and completeness which has been his in the past and will be his in the future; which, by an action of response and self-giving, can be his at any time in the present.

Thus, the man of faith feels able to live in a new way even now. He is sustained in Life Eternal. He is blessed with immediate Being. Outside his special circumstances, however, Being is experienced as belonging to the past or to the future only. With regard to the 'natural man', Sartre's claim would seem to be justified – 'abundance of being can be grasped only through the instrument of apprehension, which is the Past'; 'Essence comes from the ground of the future to the existent as a meaning which is never given and forever haunts it.'[10] *The need to recover or achieve Being is always experienced as consciousness of time.* It is the lack of synchronicity of the in-itself and the for-itself which is responsible for our existential malaise. If, somehow, they were to coincide temporally we should have that state of affairs which Sartre himself calls 'the Ideal' – an experience of *present* Being. What we so sadly lack is 'the pure possibility of a "this" to be consistent with its essence'.[10] 'Temporality divides,' says Sartre, 'unity of being and experience can only occur when time stops.' But how, we may ask, could such a thing be? The answer would seem to be that certain experiences, notably experiences of religion and art, corporate experiences of relationship and wholeness, are able in some mysterious way to overcome the distracting element in our consciousness of the passage of time, and somehow to give us time in *the present*, free from the memory and the hope which always serve to draw us away from the immediate experience of authentic existence, existence *here and now*, existence which makes no claims and has no regrets. Experiences of religion and art, the artistic expression of corporate religious belonging, act against the distracting and alienated force of temporality, and give man back to himself in the moment of present being.

We have talked about 'the time-problem of modern man'. But the problem is not really a modern one. Contemporary living seems to exaggerate it, that is all. But all man's hopes, all his aspirations, all his defeats and despairs are experiences in time. Consciousness of time brings anxiety home to man. No wonder he seeks the release of timelessness, and treasures those moments 'out of time' which are his to enjoy without surrendering the integrity of his conscious self-hood. No wonder he values those experiences by which he is increased and not decreased, moments of encounter in which there is no question of escaping into a private world of fantasy, however induced: experiences of religion and of art.

It must be admitted that as a proposition 'the stopping of time' is sheer nonsense. But it is a fair description of the experience of corporate ritual. Men attain here an awareness of a transcending truth which delivers them from the temporal ambiguity of things and events and gives life stability and permanence. Ritual has a salutory effect upon us. We realise with startling clarity that in our everyday existence we are caught up in the flux of forms so that we cannot evaluate the content of being. It is as if we do not know who or what we are because we are so concerned about the way we are attempting to be it. We lack density, we lack outline, we lack a true understanding of the mechanics of our inter-personal identity. In a word, we lack *form*. The significance of ritual is the commerce of embodied personalities, the actual, visible and tangible, demonstration of the tragi-comedy of human relationship. We are continually reminded of the facts about ourselves, our strength and weakness, our autonomy and dependence, our defining limits : The very outlines of the self become clear, our essential identity, where we begin and end; what is my own, and what defies all my best efforts at manipulation and control in order to remain obdurately somebody else's. We learn again the primal lesson, which cost us so much anguish, when as infants we were first made aware of the presence of an essential something which was somehow not ourself, an essential some-one to whom we could reach out in the urgency of our need, but whom we could not in any real or satisfactory sense *control*.

6. The Experience of Eternity

It is this re-discovery of essential factual knowledge about our-selves and our situation that stops time for us. According to von Hildebrand[13] all the functions of Christian ritual – adora-tion, praise, confession, remembrance, thanksgiving – are done in 'eternal actuality'. The act of corporate truth, the act of presence to Being, relativises the conditions of everyday exis-tence, including the consciousness of time; and this relativisa-tion is welcomed and not resented by the one whom we call the worshipper, who eagerly surrenders his own limited and compromised truthfulness, his attempts at self-knowledge and self-direction, to the revelation and presence of Truth Itself. The timeless meaning of ritual, the revelationary power of its living symbolism, shatters the worshipper's consciousness of any kind of deprivation or limitation. Now, all is achievement, all is fulfilment. In religious ritual we are in a world of absolute truth and authentic value. In the presence of Eternity, time stands still.

This is the result. But how is it achieved? That a vision of eternity should swallow up the consciousness of things temporal is straightforward enough. But how can such a vision be obtained? How can eternity be manufactured? We are brought up sharply by the self-contradiction!

First of all, eternity is not manufactured but re-called. Mircea Eliade[14] describes how rituals re-produce extra-temporal experience by recreating artistically an artificial time which serves as 'the great time'. This is 'the time before time', consisting of 'life-giving mythical events that are real and exemplary'. Ritual, in fact, serves in this way to re-make the world by interrupting in a salutory way the course of temporal events, the seemingly inevitable succession of causes and effects. But how could such a thing possibly be? First of all, we must look at 'ritual time' itself. How is it different from 'ordinary time'? Time in the 'great time' is non-teleological. Indeed, ritual is not a logical happening at all, in the sense that its reality is not tied in with the reality of everyday life, so far as everyday reality remains, inescapably, life in time. Ritual is no way logically necessary. Quite the reverse, for it represents a determined effort to abstract our essential being from the primary world of logic and causality and construct for it a secondary, but deeper, world which remains free and gratuitous. By everyday standards, this is a world which is lacking in necessity and purpose; but it is a world which is held to be both real and exemplary according to a truth deeper than the truth of everyday experience. Thus, even though ritual's interior structure may obey the rules of logic and self-consistency, its action and significance are in another dimension; they are non-propositional, non-linear.

In any other mode than its own, ritual is non-sense. But it is honest non-sense, for it lays no claim to interpretation or understanding according to a mode other than its own. It is a conscious diversion from the logical progression of events, and from the scientific causality which holds sway in the 'real world', into a new level of truth, a new kind of reality where life is shared and understood. Life-in-time obscures the truth of our being, the real facts about ourselves. New life in a nontemporal mode, allows that truth to shine clear, those facts to be recognised and assimilated.

What shall we say, then? That ritual puts men in mind of time as eternity, of real time delivered from flux and real bodies delivered from ambiguity. It is a game which offends reality in order to remind those who play it of a reality which precedes the reality which it offends. Standing apart, we may doubt the authenticity of such an experience. But for those who are taking part, the autonomy of the simply rational, the critical, the detached, has been profoundly disturbed by the act of participation in mystery. 'Ordinary' reality, the reality of everyday experience, turns out to be blessedly less than real, less than the whole truth. In the 'great time', the time which is re-produced and re-enacted in ritual all divisions are healed, all alienation brought to an end. In Eliade's words, man is 're-integrated in his original plenitude'.[14] The rite *is* openness and opportunity, 'the spiritual space in which the world of faith, or more correctly, the world disclosed by faith, penetrates every pore of our being . . .'[13] The world of the pragmatic, where reality is used as a technique, the world of having and solving problems, the world 'manipulated for fortuitous and subjective aims', is here put to rout, and men find themselves able to make 'the creative primary gesture of personality-formation, the pure gift of the self to value as such, without the commingling of anything egocentric'.[13]

This is a function of the rite as such, of the blessed game in which we discover ourselves in the presence of a reconciling and redeeming value, a reality which is felt to be capable of transcending existential divisions, and the limitations of 'real life'. Indeed the reality of life is enhanced by the rite. Ritual focuses man's life upon that value in which he discovers his own being; through ritual, in fact, men 'feed on value' – they gain concentration and awareness in a world which discourages the acknowledgement of the simplicity of saving truth, which distracts men from the vital nature of the issues at stake for them, which blurs all outlines and confuses all questions, which depends on compromise and ambiguity, which measures the world of existential possibility with the yardstick of a reductionist logic. 'The liturgy,' says von Hildebrand, 'is itself awakeness, in the highest sense of the word, and it leads all who live in it to being awake – not only to eternal things but also to transient and earthly ones.'[13]

Ritual manages to 're-actualise for a time what was the initial state of mankind as a whole'.[14] It infuses present experience, present temporal existence, with the values of eternity, by distracting man from his preoccupation with the demands and pressures of the moment, and his habitual ways of dealing with these demands and pressures. Eliade gives examples of the way in which in Shamanistic rituals 'the human condition is surpassed without being destroyed', and men return to their original stature, that of Gods and heroes. As the primordial events recounted in the myth are made ritually present, so the inner reality of the actors relates to those events in 'an atmosphere of primal union'. This, says Eliade, is 'the great healing action of mythical ritual'.[14] Outer and inner truth conform to each other as they did of yore 'in illo tempore', and man is once again united with his environment. Wholeness is experienced as a return, and the relation which we achieve in our rituals is always a primal relation.

The pattern of return, restoration, renewal, is repeated in rituals embodying the religious understanding of many cultures throughout the world. The theological justification for the ritual may differ from place to place, along with the mythic framework, but the need for cosmic renewal, for refreshment at the centre, for a 'new start', for restoring a broken relationship with God or the gods, remains everywhere the same.[8] Thus, rituals which are symbols of timelessness and stasis, of that primal harmony and repose which is both Eden and the Kingdom of Heaven, are continually being used in the service of time.

[8] 'The defiled "image of God" is here restored in men by the reception afresh of the one archetypal image, and mankind renewed and gathered into one is presented to the Father in Christ as the "one new man", his recovered "son".' Dom Gregory Dix[15] on the Eucharist, *The Shape of the Liturgy*, p. 751.

Rituals of being contribute to becoming. Like the Christian Eucharist such rituals are 'food for a journey'. We may say that they are strictly functional.

The morphology of the rite, which is to say its distinctive scenario, the events acted out in it and the order in which the various scenes which comprise it succeed one another, contributes powerfully to the message. We may say that the shape of the rite creates an atmosphere of timelessness. Indeed, there is truly a sense in which time is abolished by the rite.

But eternity is not merely the death of time, or the perpetuation of events in time, as this may be experienced in the highly charged atmosphere of rituals of religious aspiration, individual or corporate; eternity has a particular religious meaning in itself.

The eternal implies the unique presence of God. This is particularly so, of course, for Christians. For Christian sacramental ritual, the eternal nature of the rite depends on and involves the revealed truth of God's own participation in it. In the first place, the Christian's understanding of eternal things comes from his knowledge of God Himself, rather than from his appreciation of time as being infinitely renewable as this is expressed in initiatory rituals, genuinely religious as these may be. This having been said, the fact remains that the timeless atmosphere of the rite lends itself perfectly to the Christian sacraments; for these do not represent the periodic death and resurrection of the Gods of the pagan mysteries or the heroes of archaic religions, but the historic 'saving acts' of Christ, events which, because of their historical nature and not in spite of it, may only be participated in sacramentally from a position 'outside time'.

To resume, then – there is an anthropological necessity for rituals to reassure and re-establish men on their journey through time. Our own Sacraments are basically 'rites de passage'. They are examples, if from our own point of view privileged examples, of an institution which is as widespread as human nature itself, and may be only rejected if human nature is itself repudiated: that is, the public ratification of private self-hood, the marking off of a significant stage in the changing and developing pattern of an individual's relationship with his environment. They occur along the horizontal axis of human becoming, human growth and development, but their reference is to the vertical axis of relationship and being. All are therefore in a sense sacramental. They deal with the critical problems of becoming an adult male or female, of relationships within the family, and of passing into old age; in other words, with successive stages of growth into full humanness. Their corporate nature, and the wholehearted way in which they are accepted as a necessary part of living, are everywhere apparent. It has been claimed that their usefulness depends in fact upon their openness and candour, their nature as communion, which has a directly therapeutic effect. The attainment of developmental land-marks should be marked, and marked publicly.

Man has an instinct to externalise subjectivity, and to share with other people his important interior happenings. Above all, he is conscious of a need to share and proclaim his crises. The dying and rising again of the ritual experience gives men strength to face their terror of death itself, death as final and irreversible, death as absurdity and irrelevance; but it also gives them a greater ability to emerge triumphant from all the painful crises of development as a member of human society, all the 'little deaths' that mark the road towards social adjustment, and the love of neighbour and of God which marks a healthy and happy community. As Eliade says, 'If one already knows death here below, if one is continually dying countless deaths in order to be born to something else, something that does not belong to the earth but participates in the sacred, then one is living, one may say, a beginning of immortality, a growth into immortality,'[14] an immortality attained by climbing a ritual ladder to personal fulfilment and wholeness. Sometimes but not always, this is a *public* immortality, an immortality of the race. Sometimes it is the individual elevation of saintly souls out of the common destiny of mankind. The initiate is enabled to bring his inner life into the light of common day, and so to find reassurance in other people's reactions. He discovers that what is going on inside him does not make him different from other people; or if, temporarily, it does have that effect, that difference is taken into account by them in a public gesture of ratification. This urge towards openness and towards sharing experiences with others is part and parcel of the sense of belonging to the world, of the instinct to homologise outer and inner experience. The initiate shares in a potential holiness of the entire race, through its natural closeness to sacred things, its divine purpose and destiny.

Twentieth-century civilisation has lost touch with certain aspects of reality which belong to its health. Foremost among these is the understanding and contemplation of timelessness. The twentieth century 'consistently ignores eternity'.[9] Modern philosophy, says Camus, 'places its values at the end of action. They *are* not, but are *becoming*, and we shall know them fully only at the completion of history. We are placing history on the throne of God ... Nature is still there, however. She contrasts her calm skies and her reasons with the madness of men[10]' ... 'perhaps some day, when we are ready to die of ex-

[9] Camus and Eliade – along with other writers, including J. B. Priestley in his *Man and Time* – hold Western Christianity partly responsible for this, because of a certain eschatological stress which insists on the Incarnation of Christ as being Divine ratification of historicity as such. Eternity, which is man's true home, awaits him at the end of time. The fourth Gospel, with its developed pneumatology and its teaching about the presence of God in men and men in God here and now (what Dodd calls its 'realized eschatology'), is the most timeless strand of New Testament teaching. Indeed it is worth pointing out that according to Oscar Cullmann[16] (*Early Christian Worship*) this gospel actually has a special ritual significance, to the extent of being almost a handbook to the Sacraments. Here time and eternity are united in the ritual action of the Eucharist: 'he who eats my flesh and drinks my blood has eternal life and I will raise him up at the last day'. The gospel 'traces the line from the Christ of history to Christ the Lord of the community, in which the Word continually becomes Flesh' (Cullmann, p. 38). A contemporary school of New Testament scholarship attributes an origin in Jewish-Christian synagogue lections to the specific arrangement of traditions about Jesus in the Gospels. The various stories were intended, it is claimed, to be read in accordance with the calendar of public worship.

[10] *Helen's Exile.*

haustion and ignorance, I shall be able to disown our garish tombs and go and stretch out in the valley under the same light and learn for the last time what I know.'[11] This certainly comes very near to what Eliade calls 'man's need for the reactivation of sacred attitudes'. The implication is that his discovery of the 'active' sacredness of becoming, learning, developing, has carried man further and further away from the 'passive' sacredness of Being; man has 'abandoned himself to the vital hierophanies, to the enjoyments procurable from the immediate experiences of life, and turned away from the sanctities which surpass his immediate everyday needs'.[14] He feels ill at ease before many forms of manifestation of the 'archaic reality of the sacred', those elemental presences which we contemplate in the art of previous generations and other societies than our own. Our fear of death is both well known and well documented. But life itself is equally obscure to us – that is life as a discernible reality, as present being, as the scenario for experience which is immediate, valid and intense. We have difficulty in 'seeing life single and seeing it whole'. We have little respect for the given, or rather we disguise our fear of engagement under a mask of disdain for what presents itself. We can only bear to contemplate it in a reductionist way from a 'scientific' viewpoint, set in the inflexible categories of experience as past, present, or future; where the past assumes the nature of a shaping and determining mechanism which already includes the future, so that the present does not really exist at all. We have lost the art of standing still. We are purposeful, goal-orientated, emergent to the extent of almost continual movement. We are always journeying, never arriving. Perhaps what we have really lost is innocence, the ability to be as little children, to be and to become at the same time; to be *by* becoming. To be in this way is not to stagnate, it is to become properly, to become through being, not at being's expense, to repose in change, not to chase after it or fly before it. To be

[11] From *Return to Tipasa*.

as children are. 'The healthy infant just Being, as part of his Being, is randomly and spontaneously curious, exploratory, wondering, interested.'[17] Children are themselves; we, in contrast, grow away from ourselves. But surely the same thing is possible even for us, if we can free ourselves from the preoccupation, so dominant in this age, with the attempt to create being out of possessions and achievements. This is a neurotic and self-defeating project. In Wordsworth's phrase, it is a 'wretched boon'.

There remain expressions of humanness which do not involve this 'giving of ourselves away to getting and spending', however. Art and religion have been pushed out on to the fringe of our common experience. Somehow they must be brought back in again, despite that desire for usefulness and purposive action which combines for their exclusion with yet another sign of our loss of innocence, the exaltation of intellect above all other human attributes. Of all our natural powers, or aspects of our personality, our intellect is the most alienated from the body, and consequently from those figurative powers which find expression and fulfilment in art and ritual. 'Mind' has no need of such things; or so it is implied. They involve honesty, humility, candour. They involve a challenge and a reward. They demonstrate the human condition in a way which, while it makes use of its strengths and its aptitudes, is equally frank about its poverty and its limitations. The perennial assertion of mind is that we have no need to remember such things; they belong to pietism, to exercises in self-humiliation. Mind can do anything. Nature, of course, our own human nature, knows that we cannot really live without this self-knowledge. Nature, the implication is, may be safely ignored!

'Our society,' says Eliade, 'needs religious and cultural integration.' To use Tillich's phrase, we must learn to 'take anxiety into ourselves' and acknowledge its presence in ourselves and in our world. So we must re-discover ourselves as a part of a world which only makes sense if its sacredness is acknowledged, for its sacredness is the cause of our anxiety and also its cure. As Christians in particular we must re-discover the truth of the central insights of our religion, of a world delivered from meaninglessness and death, but a world 'made restless until it rests in God'. We have our being as part of nature's unknown and unknowable totality. Our sacredness – our mystery and longing, our reality – is nature's sacredness. We move towards whatever is ultimate for us, whatever summons us, in our own way.

And it must be our own way, our own natural mode of response. Our rites are the expression of our sacredness. Here we re-discover our natural identity, our truth, our meaning, to offer it to the sacred other, the unknown, the un-natural, which calls out to us, and to which, or to Whom, our hearts aspire. The movement is both outwards and inwards, outwards in response and inwards in discovery and consolidation; we dig deeper into what we ourselves are and reach out further towards what we are not. By reaching out we penetrate. We are reconciled with our own being. Rites of homologisation with nature, rites of passage through process of time, in which distance and differentiation, the essential facts of our life, are acknowledged; rites which show what we are, giving us time to re-discover ourselves in our true nature, such rites reveal us as disposable beings, beings for giving and taking, for responding to the address of otherness. The proclamation of the truth makes the truth both real and liveable. The acting out of meaning in rituals embodies and perpetuates that meaning in living flesh, giving its own sacredness to life.

'The archaic reality of the sacred.' We should not be misled by the word 'archaic'. What is archaic may still be true. The truth of the sacredness of nature is primal truth. It is the truth of the meeting of otherness, Martin Buber's 'first primary word of existence', the eternal apartness which gives life through relation. This is the Presence which is subject to no human power, no function of the human personality, and which is ignored at our peril. Human being is a reaching out in mutual responsiveness; it is 'I and Thou'; it is faith and grace; it is the word of differentiation and mutuality, the child saying 'mama' for the first time. There is no other kind of human being, and there is no other way of attaining to it other than this, the way of relation. No wonder, then, that the rites of archaic societies are rites of reconciliation with nature as sacred. For what is the sacredness of nature but the otherness of nature? And what is ritual but the reaching out to otherness? What is it but the acted realisation that, in Buber's words, we are all 'bound up in relation to the same centre',[7] to the mystery of creation? But these are rites of homologisation and relationship, not techniques of homogenisation and control. The more man strives for the mastery over his world, the more he tries to establish himself at the expense of nature, rather than in and through nature, at the expense of the other instead of in communion with the other: the more he loses his true self, the more he is alienated from his own being. Thus he quarries the stone of the world in order to build his own prison. His skill, his ingenuity, his mastery of people and things become so easily the means of his death. He cannot live in what he knows. He must discover how to devote himself to what he does not know. Between what he is and what he is not, what he knows and what he does not know, between 'here' and 'there', in the tension of becoming, man lives. This tension, this 'betweenness' is at one and the same time our alienation and our life, our reconciliation. If we reject it, it must haunt us simply because it is our truth, and belongs to our being. If we accept it, then we accept ourselves with it.

In rituals we devote ourselves to what we do not know and cannot master. We turn ourselves towards otherness, intransigence, sacredness, in the knowledge that a man must so devote himself in order to live. The rite is the symbol of our devotion. We cannot rationalise it, or give it any other kind of reality than its own symbolic reality. If we attempt this sacrilege, the rite will no longer be itself. Instead of our devotion to the unknown, it will become yet another means of self-isolation, yet another sign of self-idolatry. But in rituals the

world's identity is symbolised by the identity of separate personages valued in and for their separatedness. What better symbol of the intransigent and beckoning Other to whom we respond in relation across the gap of existence than the rite,
union of body and spirit, man and man!

4 Rite and Place
(The Rite as a Staged Encounter)

Up to now, the symbols which have been occupying our attention, either implicitly or explicitly, have been the following:
the womb which is also the tomb, the font, the monster's belly,
the clashing symplegades, the tree which connects earth and
heaven, time and eternity. This last image will carry us into
this final chapter. For it is a symbol of *relationship*, of the rite
as a place of meeting, a space for meeting. Other symbols we
might perhaps use would be the well at the world's end, seen
as a meeting place as well as an object of pilgrimage, the feast
of the Great King, the mountain or tower of divine revelation.[1]

For here we are concerned with man's reaching out towards
otherness by his construction of a place of encounter. The
simplest church of all is the circle cleared in the midst of the
crowd, in the market-place or at the corner of the street, which
is formed by simply holding people back so that they can look
across at one another and see one another while remaining a
part of the assembly; and this is also the simplest theatre.

In this chapter we will try to face the implications of this fact, and of the artistic nature of the rite itself. For the rite is very much something that is *staged*.

1. The Place of Truth

A language is a way of synthesising perception for the purpose of communication, either with the self or with other people. It is a way of collecting certain kinds of evidence for the formation of certain kinds of conclusions. Because it is a language, one of a number of languages available for organising experiences, ritual can cope with contradictory data. Indeed this is what it is *for*. The language of ritual synthesises existential discords which do not yield readily to other kinds of dialectic. This ritual synthesis is violent and gentle, as befits a code of communication with and about ultimate concern. It is a heightened language. Its violence proceeds from the force of the dialectic, the definiteness and lack of ambiguity of the presences involved; the harsh contradiction of thesis and antithesis, the difference between men and God, as this is implied in the bodily demonstration of intransigent separation and self-hood in the rite.

And yet it is this bodily presence, the clear outline of man's separation from God and division from his neighbour, that renders the rite gentle. For the body remains the soul's true instrument. Because of its concreteness, the body divides. It points the dialectical language of man and man and man and God. Because of its disposability, the body unites. It is the symbol of a loving movement of mutuality.

We are concerned here with the mutual longing of separate and autonomous universes of thought and feeling. Alone among languages the rite is privileged to set the scene for the encounter of otherness in its most radical form. What happens in this symbolic 'space for encounter' cannot happen anywhere else. The 'ritual ground', whether it be a clearing in the forest, a field on the other side of the river or any sort of sanctuary or church building, is distinguished from all other locations because of what happens there. This is the place set aside for dying in order to live, chosen to be a heaven and a hell, the scene of a cosmic or a supra-cosmic journey.

However, we are not concerned here simply with a way of expressing a certain doctrine about sanctification or death and resurrection. Initiatory rituals the world over embody the truths they preach, and are not intellectual propositions. In the progression myth–symbol–rite, dogma is by-passed. There is no possibility of intellectual error because no propositional statement is made. The movement from myth to ritual via symbol constitutes the primary form of religious expression. It is to be found in all religions which recognise a higher and more perfect reality than the common reality of everyday, a reality to which men may instinctively aspire, whatever doctrinal rationale they may give to their actions.

For the immediate, non-thetic, existential meaning of the symbol is quite clear. Among animals, birds, fishes, rituals fulfil necessary functions of communication. Attitudes, and more especially relationships, which cannot be transmitted by verbal symbols, can be embodied in ritual. Changes of relationship, information about intentions, are frequently signalled in this way. We may instance the mating rituals of various species of birds and fish, in which ritual battles are 'played' rather than fought. The object here is the acknowledgement by the family, tribe or flock, of the emergent sexual and social significance of one of its members, rather than the achievement of an actual victory. The death of a rival is not the desired end so much as the recognition of the victor's new role in society, his new position in the 'pecking order'. This kind of ritual is the type of all non-propositional communication. Anti-social behaviour is used to signal a social intention; the 'acted reality' of death promotes the cause of life. All this is at a level more primitive, more explicit, and somehow deeper and more salutory than description. In the acting-out of intentions, all the behavioural variables are demonstrated, as in a spoken language the range of possibilities is expressed in the contrast and alignment of propositions. Indeed, the rite is a demonstration of new reality in all its urgency, with all its implications, a new state of affairs within the community. The integrity of society is maintained without the disruptions of an actual battle and a real death. But the battle and the death are *there*, nonetheless. The rite is both defensive and offensive, a safeguard against violence and an assertion of the triumph of newness, the force of new life over the balance of conflicting claims and rivalries which preserves the status quo within the group. At this basic level, ritual serves to show the whole existential picture, when the literal content of that wholeness involves difficulties which put it beyond the scope of any other kind of presentation.

Man's anxiety, say the existentialist psychologists, is rooted in his inability to use his freedom responsibly; to use it in engagement with the world, and so catch up with his own being which somehow belongs in the world. The nature of this belonging is more paradoxical than logical. It cannot be mere conformity, which is a surrender of personal truth. It must be that much more difficult and elusive thing which we call relationship. The fact which always clamours for attention is the fact of distance. It is distance which produces anxiety – but it is distance which also underlies and permits relation. In human relationship man reaches out for man across the gulf of his own and the other's existential isolation. The isolation of persons, regarded as persons, allowed to be persons, is such that they cannot lose their identity, they cannot be swamped, incorporated, reduced, *known*. They can only be encountered. They can only be touched. *Twentieth-century literature leads us to believe that of all generations our own is most aware of the politics of relationship*. And yet, as we have seen, the twentieth century is the age of alienation.

Our consciousness of our own alienation takes many forms. It occurs as a protest against the pressure of life, the sheer noise and bustle of life in our society, its preference of 'outwardness' to 'inwardness'; 'ages no longer related to silence like the modern age do not bother about the ontic in things. They are concerned only with the profitability, the exploitability, and

the revolutionary possibilities in things ... With our foundations in Being thus weakened we are cut off from the possibility
of forming deep human relationships.'[2] It occurs also in the
frequency with which modern society is diagnosed by social
psychologists as 'schizoid'. 'In the nineteenth century,' says
Eric Fromm, 'the problem was that *God is dead*; in the twentieth
century the problem is that man is dead. In the nineteenth
century inhumanity meant cruelty; in the twentieth century
it means schizoid self-alienation. The danger of the past was
that men became slaves. The danger of the future is that men
may become robots ...'[3] 'external anxiety and guilt have
lessened', says Rollo May, 'but *internal* anxiety and guilt have
increased. And in some ways these are more morbid, harder to
handle, and impose a heavier burden upon the individual than
external anxiety and guilt.'[4] The alienation of society is held
to be a kind of generalised schizophrenia, a kind of 'withdrawal-
insanity'. 'Schizophrenia and alienation are complementary. In
both forms of sickness one side of human experience is lacking.
The person who is in touch only with his inner world and
who is incapable of perceiving the outer world in its objective
action context, is insane. The person who can only experience
the outer world photographically, but is out of touch with his
inner world, with himself, is the alienated person.'[5] In the
alienated person, product of the alienated society, there has
occurred a general draining away of the richness and the realism
of human experience. Such a person has suffered what the existential psychologists call a 'meaning-loss'. The relationship between himself and his own world of people and things has
ceased to be a true relation. He is no longer established in his
own being by his awareness of the being of others; instead, he
is shut away in existential solitude behind crash-barriers which
he himself has laboriously erected. There is a collusion here
between tendencies of self-preservation which are infantile, unadaptive, and therefore 'pathological', and the pressures of a
rejecting society itself bent on self-assertion and self-preservation, the exercise of power without responsibility, a society cut

off from its own being and at odds with its own truth, which refuses to acknowledge its essence as human relationship, the commerce of interpersonal giving and receiving.

Eliade describes how in corporate rituals, man becomes fully human. It is his nature to aspire towards a more spiritual modality and to incorporate his experience within himself. At such moments 'time stands still' and he is present to eternal Being. But it does this in any presentation of the essential truth about the human condition. The essential truth about human wholeness is contained in the act of reaching out, the 'model moment of relationship', which constitutes the 'breaking of the tension between the self and other'. This is the moment of love, the act of creation, in which the terms of the encounter with otherness are laid down for us by the very limits of our own personality, limits made explicit by our own bodies, the symbols of our separation and identity. Our bodies demonstrate relationship in the changing dispositions of a ritual dance. Our use of them in song and silence, gesture and stillness, dance and solemn movement, provides that distance between persons, that obdurate and inescapable self-ness, which is overcome in the movement of relationship, and upon which the possibility of relation, as such, depends. The dance divides and unites, alienates and reconciles, weaves its own patterns, loses its co-herence only to find it again, achieves unity and balance in terms of disunity and haphazardness. In a strange way which is more truthful than thinking and feeling, the dance demonstrates the facts of life. Thus relationship uses the forms of art to reveal itself. Because it itself is the achievement of unity and encounter by means of disunity and separation, it is able to demonstrate itself in the emergence of order from chaos, the expression of meaning in terms of meaninglessness, and truth in terms of artifice, which we call a work of art. Art becomes the perfect medium of religious awareness once it is understood that the work of art depends upon, that it lives in and through, separation.

2. The Truthfulness of Artefacts

Both Eliade and von Hildebrand relate the ultimacy of ritual truth, the final value of the ritual language, to a specific experience of timelessness. Myth, says Eliade, is absolute truth in that it recounts events in a sacred history which transcends and out-values ordinary history. Thus the rite 'makes men into Gods' by lifting them out of profane time with its errors and limitations. The explicit reference in the person and acts of the mythical hero to a special sort of time, in which time itself is transcended, certainly contributes to the experience of timeless truth in corporate rituals, but it does not adequately explain that experience. How in fact is this 'special sort of time' restored to men? Myth *by itself* is not enough to do this, for the secret is to be found not in exposition but in relationship. What we are concerned with here is myth in relation to absence, the symbol that proclaims its own inadequacy and so points away from itself without any confusion of subject and object. It is the artistic nature of ritual that alone can give us the clue to ritual's timelessness and its ability to mediate Eternity to man in symbolic action. For the more 'contrived' and gratuitous the symbol is, the greater its power to direct us towards its partner in relationship, to that which stands over against it – to that truth which calls out to us, which we may apprehend, and to which we respond, but which we may neither grasp wholly nor attempt to manipulate.

True art is relational; it is the expression of a relational aesthetic, the mirror of a relational theology. Dorothy Sayers[6] has pointed out that so long as we cling fast to a platonic doctrine of God the ontology of art is indeed suspect, for it can be nothing more than the imitation of an imitation, human reality being itself not a relation to God but an imitation of Him. Art, then, is 'a cheating imitation of the visible world', a world which itself is 'only a pale reflection of the heavenly realities'. This attitude, that art is a cheat and consequently a distraction from, and dissipation of, the life of moral obedience and ethical commitment, is shared by as Christian a writer as Kierke-gaard.[7] Indeed, it is the classical Protestant view of art. This kind of art has a certain therapeutic value. Certainly, it is an attempt to manipulate the spectator by a process of imaginative involvement. But equally certainly it may have the effect that Aristotle[8] claims for it, it may 'take us out of ourselves' in a movement of sympathetic self-giving, an impulse of involve-ment, towards some other person, even if that other person is a personage artificially contrived as a *meeting-place* between artist and spectator. Even this 'kathartic' art, the art of the 'staged' meeting and the artificially induced encounter can promote relationship, while remaining non-relational in its own essential nature.

But the art which involves us against our will or distracts us against our will, the art which does not leave us free to choose, free to bestow ourselves or withhold ourselves, can never achieve the dignity of art which needs no justification in terms of the artist's benevolent intention of instruction or entertain-ment. True art, archetypal art, lacks this element of coercion or indoctrination. True art is neither trivial nor seductive, neither a distraction nor a snare. It is no kind of instrument at all. It promotes freedom of response to something *new*. *It reaches towards the other in relationship, an expression or an action of being rather than having or doing.* All ideas of force and subjugation – of, for example, the painful synthesis of content and form as in the aesthetic doctrine of Hegel, or Nietzsche's upsurge of Dionysiac feeling in opposition to the direction of the Appollonian intellect – detract from the uniqueness of the true work of art, which is not something made any more than it is something copied. The true work of art *emerges*. It proceeds *from* a relation, *in* a relation. Its theology, that is its ultimate ontological truthfulness, is no less than the Christian theology of Creation. This is what Dorothy Sayers says about it: 'Sup-pose that, having rejected the words "copy", "imitation", and "representation" as inadequate, we substitute the word "Image", and say that what the artist is doing is to "*image forth*" something or the other, and connect this with St Paul's phrase "God has spoken to us by His Son, the brightness of His glory, and the express image of His person ..." The truth, the idea, (that is to say, the artist's *experience*), and its expression in the work of art are separable and yet they are the same. The second is the image of the first, but the first is not to be thought of except as the second,'[6] i.e. except as a new creation; but having emerged, the image stands forth as revealing the experience in terms of itself, which are the only possible terms of its revelation. In coming forth thus, the image is recognised by the artist as both itself, something quite new, and also as his original idea or experience, incarnated now in a material body which is capable of awakening recognition in the beholder in a new relationship of address and response, a new encounter of otherness.[1] In the light of the Christian doctrine of God, art is no imitation but a demonstration of divinity in the act of giving itself to man in the Incarnation. Newness is bodied forth in relation as itself, and yet it has no separate being apart from that relation. It is not a technique to be used for any set purpose but an image of relationship standing between an artist and his fellow men, a place of relation and meeting. Its truth is neither imposed nor denied: it emerges.

Art and theology are brought together as parallel analogies of Divine action. This has of course been done before, notably by Freidrich Hegel;[9] but whereas in the doctrine of Hegel this action is the forceful subjugation of the world of the flesh by Divine Spirit, what is mirrored forth here is the loving act of God's encounter with men in a relationship of genuine union, a really Christian Incarnation. We are reminded of the 'aesthetic theology' of Martin Buber. To Buber, art is a symbol of human existence, of the oscillation of the 'I'–'Thou' and the 'I'–'It', of the conceptualising awareness which emerges again

[1] 'The act of the poet in creation is seen to be three-fold – a trinity – experience, expression, and recognition; the unknowable reality in the experience; the image of that reality known in its expression; and power in the recognition; the whole making up the simple and indivisible act of creative mind.' D. L. Sayers, *Unpopular Opinions*, p. 39.

and again as a non-thetic responsiveness in the beholder. 'In bodying forth I disclose; I lead the form which confronts me across into the world of "It". The work produced is a thing among things, able to be experienced and described as a sum of qualities. But from time to time it can face the receptive beholder in its whole embodied form . . .'[10] The artist takes the quality of otherness, that which is 'over against', and lives 'in relation'; by taking it he banishes its quality of otherness into a temporary exile, from which it is able to emerge from time to time 'inspiring and blessing'. The moment of its emerging is a 'timeless moment'.[10]

For, in the artistic event, content and form draw near each other to become an incarnational unity, in which both partners remain distinct while being wholly united. In ritual the work of art is 'man-in-relationship'. This is the ' "It" which endlessly becomes "Thou" again', the true embodiment of spirit, man's valid symbol of himself. 'Man-in-relationship' is the art form which is human personality, whose content is the embodied human presence and whose form is the body's freedom of address and response. Life, meaning, human truthfulness, come from the meeting of persons in which each responds to other, and the spirit of man encounters that which is over against him in a responsive and transforming happening. Corporate ritual, the acted rite, bears witness to an acceptance of, and embodies a proclamation about, the reality of relation as the mode of human being. In it, we offer our whole selves as responsiveness to the Other who confirms us in being, establishing us as ourselves, blessing us body and soul.

This is what Marcel means when he says that 'the rite gives rhythm to fidelity'. Our bodily actions, our use of mythological expressions to embody the meaning of men and God, symbolise a total giving of self, soul and body, a total 'disposability' to the Other. 'Ours is a being whose concrete essence is to be in every way involved.'[11] Not merely the sign, but the actual means of this involvement is my body, which I both am and have; which, in relationship, I give. The symbol of my body's free responsiveness to God is the ritual action in which I demonstrate my disposability to otherness and my consequent achievement of being. This is not achieved by any denial of existential isolation, of the separation between man and his world, and man and himself. Indeed, it is *by accepting isolation and separation as fact* that relationship is achieved in rituals. This uniqueness of personal self-hood, this stubborn 'otherness' of the self, provides that distance between existence and being, between our actual human life and our ideal life of union and of belonging, which permits them to come together in an 'artistic' relation of content and form. Distance dictates the terms of the encounter of otherness and allows the response which is our freedom and our life. This is the honesty of art; it acknowledges the difficulty of relation, it emerges from the hard outlines of our existential separation, it proceeds from what Buber calls 'The stern over-againstness of "I" and "Thou".'[12]

For in ritual, our alienation is not denied but acknowledged, even proclaimed. Art, which emerges from the fact of distance and the apartness that permits relation, provides us with a potent symbol, a symbol which includes both the nature of our disease and the demonstration of its cure. This simultaneous acceptance of wholeness and infirmity, deprivation and restoration, banishment and home-coming, does not belong to 'ordinary' time. In our daily lives we are only able to experience one basic existential emotion at a time. But for man in his alienated condition, this paradoxical and contradictory way of being carries with it a very powerful feeling of authenticity, when it is encountered in the timeless atmosphere of ritual; he is aware of a strange honesty and 'rightness', a sense of being able to acknowledge a saving truth about himself and the world, to which at other times and in other places he is somehow blind.

Any salve for our disunity, our schizoid condition, is likely to share this quality of acceptance of discord and diversity, the 'co-incidentia oppositorum', which religion shares with art. In terms of compromise, or of unilateral capitulation, no satisfactory conclusion may be arrived at. The division must be transcended. It cannot be denied. The facts about our human condition must be given expression. Even when the gestures of the actor are allowed no metaphysical significance, as with Camus, comfort may be derived from the acted proclamation of human-ness. We value the symbolic, acted expression of truth, even if the truth is absurdity. How are we to explain this reconciliation where there is no faith, no objective doctrine of healing, neither the acceptance nor the rejection of rationality?

The rite itself has power. The rite transcends the problem of meaning and the limitation of intellectual understanding. It locates the unknown. By mapping the possibility of future meaning it not only records experience but extends it. It embodies aspiration within the immediate and makes what is reached after a part of present reality. For what is sought for and received is a closer relationship to the Other. He who takes part in the rite acknowledges the value of the presence of other people in his world and so acknowledges his own value to other people. He recognises the existence of the non-thetic, non-propositional world of relation. He surrenders certain long-cherished notions, the result of years of tendentious instruction of what constitutes meaning for human beings. His participation marks his discovery that his existential discomfort may be shared and that the sharing is somehow redemptive. Thus men find fellowship in the very absurdity which divides them, as they recognise themselves in one another, and come to act out that fundamental understanding which they can find no other way of expressing, that relational truth which defies argument and eludes analysis.

At the centre of the rite's reconciling action is mystery, the haunting mystery of the human body itself. This is the presence that defies all reductionism, and stands forth as the unavoidable evidence of otherness, the proof of the possibility of relation between selves. In a world where relationship is the life of men, no individual person can heal his own existential pain. Whatever he knows, in the sense of comprehending, he makes his own. The gift of life itself, the mystery of relation, becomes the letter of his law, the mechanics of his awareness, a part, in other words, of himself. Looking at himself, examining his situation, he is confirmed in his loneliness. His healing must come from what he does *not* know, as the wind that blows wherever it wishes: He is delivered from himself by the thing – the presence – that he cannot control. Thus, the rite is a living paradigm of Buber's 'two-fold movement basic to man, the primal setting at a distance and entering into relation . . .'[10] Whatever there is of human truth, truth about relationship, in art, is amplified and expanded in the rite, which is a blossoming symbol of human encounter, of the 'polar unity of feeling'.[12] The mysterious circumstance of the relation-of-otherness finds here its true symbol in the factual, irreducible presence of human bodies, each unique, each distinct and separate, reaching out towards the other in the primitive gesture of fellowship and solidarity. The mystery remains a mystery. The body stands forth as the symbol of that disposable intransigence, that presence which is established in being not by clinging to itself but by giving itself away, and which finds itself as it looks for meaning in the other.

Art, says Lessing, 'offers us appearance as reality, absent things as present; it deceives and the deceit is pleasing'.[2] But art is not deceitful – it is a candid attempt to span the distance between two realities, the reality of present experience and the reality of imagined, recollected or envisaged experience, and to imbue the latter with the qualities of the former. Of these two realities, only the first is time-bound and obeys the laws of everyday logic; the second infects it with freedom and fertility according to the measure of its innate powers. The potency of shared imagination, of a common hope or purpose, of a covenant relationship, is very great indeed. In religious rituals, the 'artistic appearance' is the symbol of an overriding reality which breaks through the barriers of our reductionist logic, making 'absent'

[2] Lessing: *Laocoon*, Dent, p. 3.

things really 'present', 'in spirit and in truth'. The use of artistic contrivance honestly expresses our own circumscribed and contrived existence, which is part of the reality symbolised by the rite. Our worshipping bodies mirror exactly the conditioned spontaneity of creatureliness, while our true freedom finds expression in our use of our compromised and limited personalities, in their embodied 'this-ness' and 'here-ness', as a means of showing forth the desire to do the work of God in acts of worship. What is true of Christian worship is true of any corporate ritualised expression of a shared understanding, any ritual acknowledgement of an overriding truth about men and the world. Out of the material of our own limitation and disunity, the given circumstances of our everyday world, the having and getting which belong to our bodies, we fashion in corporate rituals a place of truth, a limitless vision of novelty, opportunity, and hope. Ritual's true nature is to be corporate, courageous, candid; and so to be a special symbol of, and occasion for, human relationship. As we have seen, human relationship is itself difficult and contradictory, involving at one and the same time the overcoming of distance and its preservation, and this again is why it finds its best analogy in that coming together of content and form which we call the artistic symbol.

3. The Theatre of Existence

In *Rite and Man*, Bouyer[13] draws attention to the close interdependence in ritual of rite and myth. The ritual actions, and the narrative framework that supports and interprets them – and is itself supported and interpreted by them – evolve as partners together. Myth and rite are the embodiment of the original word of response and recognition for men as men. As religion itself is 'the spontaneous response which man's existential situation elicits as soon as (it) is fully accepted in its reality', so a rite may be held to be 'that action in which man feels he is sharing in the divine activity'. Rite and myth, in fact, both proceed from an encounter with divinity; both are expressions of the original word of response to the wholly Other.

Thus a 'rite' (i.e. actions + myth) 'is not simply one type of action amongst many others. It is *the typical human action*, inasmuch as it is connected with the word as the expression and realization of man in the world, and to the degree that this expression and realization are immediately and fundamentally religious.'[13] Action, however, predominates over myth, only in the sense that it is the action itself that constitutes the ritual symbol which transmits and contains the rite's primal meaning, which cannot be communicated in any other way. The function of the mythical clothing is, according to Bouyer, to anchor the perception of sacred things which proceeds from the rite itself, those sacred powers and presences set free by the rite, firmly into a philosophical framework of religion. The myth, in other words, serves to provide the ritual action with its terms of reference; and without myth, we are told, a rite soon becomes simply magic.

For the myth makes the demonstration relevant to the special circumstances of our life in time. It provides the historic framework for timelessness. Mythic ritual is being expressed as becoming. It is a language about eternity that time can understand; that *we* can understand. Caught up in a flux of forms, we cannot evaluate the content of our experience or see its truth. Somehow we must be enabled to focus upon essentials, upon the essential. Out of the obvious contrivance, the purposeful limitations of the rite comes insight into the truth about ourselves, that we can only attain true self-hood, true being, by embracing contingent being in all awareness of its contingency. Truth is apprehended, when limitation is acknowledged; eternity is reached, in a 'rite of passage'. True ritual, then, contains a word and a sacred action which involve us, draw us in, to make us free *from* time and consequently, free *for* time. It does this as freedom and newness emerge time and again from structure in the work of conscious art.

If, however, the myth becomes over-developed, so as to constitute a developed theology in itself, it can strangle the rite and deprive ritual of its primitive truthfulness. The extreme result of this process can be seen at various times in the history of religions. Bouyer devotes a long section of *Rite and Man* to the futile attempts of Greek philosophy to 'explain' the mystery religions. This, he says, only succeeded in depriving them of their original power, which belonged in fact to their having no explanation. Late medieval Christian ritual suffered in a similar way. Here, however, rite and explanation were not only alienated from each other, but also from those who were allegedly taking part in the ritual itself,[3] both priest and people. The movements towards liturgical reformation (both that of the sixteenth century and that now under way in the Roman Catholic Church) strive successfully to reduce this medieval opacity in the direction of greater theological explicitness; but the movement in favour of intellectual clarity seems only to undermine the power of the symbol, the direct and immediate apprehension of the worshippers' religious identity. 'Words which convey nothing more than a reasoning process in which objective reality is practically denied by the mind, which substitutes its own activity for it, and actions which no longer make sense since the gestures are so buried in the matter that no mind can penetrate them, cannot be united into an effective ritual.'[13] Word and rite 'must not be blindly opposed to each other'. Neither should they penetrate and inter-penetrate so as to become simply confused. Bouyer talks of 'restoring a mysterious density to both words and actions'. They should remain not 'opposed', but 'in juxtaposition'. In other words, they should be *in relation*.

Myth and rite, imagination and performance, mind and body are partners in all ritual. Basically, ritual is a story and some actors, an intention and some bodies. Which gives life to the rite? Both. Both myth and action together, or rather in their relationship, give ritual its special life, its unique identity. On

[3] 'The tendency was to make the liturgy something that took on the character of the incomprehensible, something which the people assisted at but in which they had no part, something which issued from the hands of the priests, but like some prodigy which escaped even him.' *Rite and Man*, p. 58.

the one hand, there is the life of the body, the disposition of living flesh, thoughts, intuitions, emotions, intentions, preferences – both mental and physical – decisions, impulses; on the other the life of shared imagination, memory, determination, hope. Myth is usually given pre-eminence over ritual action because of the imagination's power to people its creations from out of its own substance. As G. S. Kirk has shown, myth does not need ritual although ritual must involve myth, even if it is merely the myth of the world's meaninglessness and man's absurdity. As we have seen ourselves it is the strange disposability of the human body itself, the myth-making actor who is at one and the same time imagination and circumstance, freedom and structure, form and content, which constitutes the life of corporate ritual. But the myth of the ancient hero who lives again, the paradisal time which is made present is the very rock upon which the rite is founded. It is the intransigent material with which our corporeality allies to produce the given circumstances of the ritual happening, the rite's unique scenario. It gives to the work of art its hard outlines. In order to assert the ultimate force of its own truth, the rite sets itself the hardest possible tasks to overcome. In leaping the barriers of space and time its actors demonstrate the triumph of relationship, and turn the ritual ground into an ideal meeting of otherness. It is in this ideal relation of action and word, present and past, rite and myth, that ritual declares itself as art.

The particular art-form involved is, quite straightforwardly, theatre. Indeed, there are signs that in twentieth-century Western society, theatrical experience has come to resemble most clearly the experience of corporate ritual. This is not really surprising, however. Both corporate religious ritual and theatrical performance share a common basic identity. Both symbolise the relation of form and content, rationalisation and happening, mind and body which constitutes the authentic human mode of being in the world. Both possess the quality of 'presentness' which we examined in the last chapter, the power to synchronise past and future, the experience as it approaches us and our understanding of that experience, the act of reaching out and the act of incorporating and living. One truth lies at the heart of both, the truth of relation. It is this truth that they first demonstrate in their own working, and then allow to work in the world at large. If this common identity is not everywhere apparent – and indeed it is not, nor has it ever been – the fault lies, not in the things themselves, but in our misuse of them. What so many object to in religious ritual is not ritual at all, but a distortion of ritual, the 'character it assumes when it begins to degenerate'. Specifically, a distortion of its relational truth. In theology, it is a tendency to confuse an opportunity of meeting and encounter with the Wholly Other, undertaken in obedience and gratitude, with a selfish attempt to abrogate power and impose will. In psychology, it is a concentration on the distortion that ritual undergoes when it is deprived of its content of 'the other' and encounters only the self. In anthropology it is a persistent misunderstanding of the linguistic function of corporate rites, or the determination to regard them as a code of social organisation rather than the authentic language of religious awareness.

We might say, in fact, that each of these disciplines sees ritual as wholly formal, as the enemy of content, life, freedom, and attacks it as such. But ritual exists in the artistic relation of content and form, in which what is familiar, ordinary, domestic, responds to the challenge of what is new, strange, alien, just as self-hood responds to otherness. To see it in any other way is to look at it in a distorting mirror of some kind. In its true identity, it is a means of encounter. As such, it is necessarily corporate: It is necessarily undemanding, in the sense that it allows the other *to be* the other. It is necessarily honest and candid, for deception inhibits the meeting of selves. All these qualities it shares with theatre; for the play also depends on meeting and cannot therefore be primarily either a deception or a manipulation. As Guillaume Apollinaire says, to be itself, theatre can never be mere 'trompe l'œil'.

In other words, the play and the rite are bad theatre and bad ritual when they are bad art; when they do not allow the meeting of free persons in their freedom. It is for its theatrical nature that religious ritual has been attacked by theologians; but it is the common element in theatre and corporate ritual which is the ultimate justification of both. This is their nature as art and their identity as meeting. In neither is there any original idea of force or of subjugation or the imposition of the will. They are the meeting that produces meeting. Only art can properly embody such an encounter so that its nature can reproduce itself in the lives of men, for art is the potent symbol of encounter.

Thus the artistic or theatrical nature of ritual serves to produce a special 'atmosphere for encounter', in which we are enabled to meet one another and so discover ourselves as we really are. The rite provides what Antonin Artaud has called 'the structure in time for that meeting for which the being of man ceaselessly cries out, but which in life it can so rarely achieve'.[14] The aboriginal tribes of Australia use the word 'alcheringa', or 'dream time' to refer to that sacred time of the world's beginnings, in which men, women, and beasts lived together in a perfect society. The meaning of the word has spread, however, to include not only that special time and its representation in ritual, but also the place where it is represented, the 'sacred ground' set aside outside the camp. In this way the 'dream time' becomes an actual location, a 'dreaming-place', where men act out in corporate rituals the truths which guide and inspire them, both their theatre and their sanctuary.

4. *Myth and Movement*

So-called 'primitive' societies are willing to recognise the spiritual importance of encounter to the extent of ritually changing the outside world to accommodate the growing individual by reproducing his interior crises in a form both exterior and public. Van Gennep's[15] book is full of descriptions of this. The rites of passage he describes have a direct meaning, in the sense that they are descriptive and pictorial and not prescriptive and hidden. As was pointed out in Chapter 2, they represent a shared view of the world of men and things, a reality in which inner and outer, individual and corporate, the world and its inhabitants, are brought into alignment, rather than merely reproducing the features of some interior landscape. Their action is primarily one of reconciliation or harmonisation, rather than of therapeutic self-expression or ab-reaction. They are held to be sacred because their fundamental importance is recognised, not because they are secret and magical, only to be understood by a select few. Existence itself is felt to be sacred; and 'transitions from one group and from one social situation to the next are regarded as implicit in the very fact of existence. The universe itself is governed by a periodicity which has repercussions on human life, with stages and transitions, movements forward and periods of relative inactivity.'[15]

The psychological, psychosomatic, power of the social and the corporate is widely acknowledged by anthropologists. Van Gennep in particular stresses the social aetiology of significant events which are often given a physiological or a psychological, in the sense of intra-psychic, rationale, events which constitute critical stages in the individual life-cycle; puberty, marriage, pregnancy, childbirth, death, mourning.[4] Thus the individual develops hand in hand with his role in society, and does not inflict his development upon a culture which is at odds with individuality, a repressive and reductionist environment. By its corporate rituals, says van Gennep, society sets the individual free to develop, giving him its powerful blessing in the new stage of his life. What has long been denigrated as magic is now recognised as social truth. At each stage of his life the

[4] Circumcision, for instance, he holds to be an act of sociological, and not primarily physiological, significance. Social expectations take primacy over actual bodily changes in producing the state of mind of the initiate. Circumcision and actual puberty do not occur at the same time in many cultures.

developing person is led by his elders into a deeper understanding of the interdependence of himself and other people. He learns the truth about society and social organisation, and he does so at a level which actively promotes his personal health and happiness. Rites have no other meaning apart from this specifically inter-personal one; but this meaning gives cohesion to all corporate ritual. The shape of the rite reveals the shape of society; and the thing that emerges so clearly and consistently from all ritual experience of this kind is the revelation of man's awareness of belonging to his particular environment, his partnership with nature in all the exaltations, vicissitudes, tragedies, and renewals of life as growing and changing. 'Between a multiplicity of forms either consciously expressed or merely implied, a typical pattern always recurs. The pattern of the rites of passage.'[15] Because the 'passage' is real it must be acknowledged in ritual involving a real journey, real movement from one place to another. The rites identify social and psychological movement with territorial movement, because that alone is actually demonstrable. In fact, those taking part are moved into another existential location. The individual or the group to be introduced into the new situation proceed out of the old place into the new one via an intermediate stage which is neither old or new. This is the stage, common to all corporate rituals, which concerned us in the last section, the time of dying, the inevitable crucial period upon which new life wholly depends. It involves a sojourn either alone or with other initiates in 'paradise', a womb-like environment, a time of pain and safety, which brings forth new life into the world. Van Gennep points out that the rite's sacredness subsists in the special status of those taking part, who are still in the world of men, but at a deeper level than common humanity, closer to the undifferentiated being of nature. The natural world, he says, is believed to possess an inner sacredness which communicates itself to those who participate in rituals of corporate solidarity. In such rites man is reconciled to man because he is united to that natural being of the world which includes and supports both him and his neighbour, the experience of which removes inter-personal tensions and individual anxieties.

But it is not man's destiny to be part of the world of nature, but to transcend that world. And it is an over-simplification of the role of corporate ritual to suggest that it functions in accordance with a simple alignment of human aspirations and needs with the restorative 'sacrality of nature', or of man's cultural awareness with the harsh realities of the natural world, as van Gennep suggests. The rite's meaning is expressly and exclusively religious, in that, through the ritual scenario, a more developed and 'higher' expression of human person-hood emerges from the state of undifferentiated existence which corresponds to life before birth, as this presents itself to the conscious imagination of the participants. Out of this acted idea, this ritual return to the state of a fœtus in the corporate womb of the race, is born a more integrated notion of self-hood, a greater sense of being a free agent, separate and responsible, emergent in the world – and consequently, a truer relationship towards other people.

The rite actualises a society of free persons, not by merging the individual with his surroundings in an enveloping holiness of nature, but by isolating him from those surroundings, by as it were, setting him off against them, in a contrast of values and holiness. This is the religious nature of the rite, in which the new man bursts forth from the pupa of his old self, and reaches out in a new independence of spirit to offer the gift of love, the gift of *himself*, and achieve the goal of union and perfection.

Here, then, art and religion go hand in hand, 'We can only see the sacredness of the world when we discover it is a divine play.' What is noticeable in plays is a sharply developed sense of the individuality of the personages represented and their relationship, rather than any merging of identity in the supra-personal or universal; if the universal is present it is present in terms of the personal. It reveals itself as persons, *between* persons.

5. *Rite and Faith*

Christians believe that what draws man to man is not the 'natural being of the world' but the grace of God. But it must be emphasised that everywhere in human society, the rite plays the same role in reconciling man to his fellow creatures and to the circumstances of his life in the world. It is the rite's nature to be fundamentally ambiguous. To be, at one and the same time, 'in' time and 'out of' it. It is, of course, its function in linking disparate partners together that renders it ambiguous. The cultus serves to bind men to the reality which eludes them, whether that reality be of this world or of some other order; whether 'eternal truth' be the truth of God or nature. The time-wards or historic identity of ritual must remain especially precious to Christian people, as it did to the Jews of the Old Testament. Eichrodt draws attention to the significance of the Israelite amphictyony in 'keeping alive the realization that the Covenant was rooted in history and bound up with a new order of life'. The Jewish Cultus 'resisted any attempt to dissolve the covenant concept in the timelessness of myth'.[16] For Jew and Christian alike ritual establishes the immediate reality of revelation by *locating* it – on a definite day, to be remembered and relived; in specific objects, which according to God's assurance, transmit, under sacramental forms, the presence and power of Divinity – the law, the Ark, the bread and wine, the waters of baptism. The idea involves no limitation of the scope of Divine Revelation. Quite the contrary, for the historicisation of God's presence, whether it be His presence *then*, at the time of the original theophany, or *now* in the ritual action of the cultus, serves as a point of departure for the divinisation of all reality which is temporal and spatial. 'Here' and 'now' is the message of the cultus – and therefore 'everywhere' and 'at all times'.

Thus the 'time-out-of-time' may serve as a kind of trans-temporal ratification of human history. There is a sense, indeed, in which ritualistic religion, *by its very concentration on time-*

lessness, gives a greater value to immediate reality than any religion that rejects rituals. As we saw in the very first section of this book, the purpose of Christian ritual is to ratify and establish human things by relating them, not in terms of an idea, a formula, or a piece of wishful thinking, but by a gift, a presence, to the things of God, the timeless and spaceless reality of Heaven. We may now say that this is not true only of Christian ritual, but of all religious ritual. This is the basic function of corporate ritual, to give a reality which is held to be secondary the blessing of one which is held to precede it; to give men the blessing of nature, to give finitude the blessing of the infinite, to give the individual the blessing of community. In ritual, a man comes home, he returns to a primal richness and satisfaction; and because home is *really* home, when he emerges again to continue his wanderings he does so refreshed and renewed, in mind, body, and spirit.

The drawing near to each other of the ultimate and the conditioned, which presents itself as an approach on the part of the infinite rather than an abrogation of power, or an assumption of dignity, by finitude, does not make ultimacy less ultimate, or take away its inspiring quality, its life-giving, challenging, otherness. Quite the opposite. At this point, it is as well to repeat what was said in Chapter 2 about the Christian Eucharist, that the sense of the immanence of God is in no way at the expense of His holiness; the holiness of God shines forth in the cultus at once safeguarded and exposed by the nature of ritual as art, which does not allow the possibility of confusion between subject and object, and which distances the symbols of ultimacy in order to underline their essential symbolic provenance. And yet at the same time, because it is the function of art to proclaim relationship by establishing separateness, to permit mutuality by creating distance, and to encourage the self for its encounter with otherness by demonstrating the terms which are binding upon all such encounter (terms which disallow ego-centricity). Ultimate Truth, the Unconditioned, the Totally Other who is object and symbol of all search and ground of all being and growth, who alone can give unity and completeness, here becomes more and not less personal. His nearness becomes apparent through contemplation of His distance; because it is only in His distance that He can be perceived. Perceived as distant, He is known as immediate. Thus God's holiness, demonstrated in symbolic ritual, demonstrated by the necessity for such a symbol of otherness and difference, *becomes* His immanence, because it becomes *the truth of relationship with Him*. Indeed, it is true to say that the rite is the externalisation of a profound insight about Divinity; for what is involved here is a basic component of the religious consciousness – the *simultaneous* comprehension of the self-made gulf which separates the soul from God, and God's welcoming love which summons the soul to itself, calling out to it across the void. This, of course, is an observation based on Christian experience; but that the rite is a symbol of truth-in-relationship, or 'truth through the relation of otherness' remains true for other cultures and cultuses than our own.

Ritual is immanent truth; and, as such, supplies men with life, *in* the present, *for* the future. Not all religious world-views accept the possibility of such a sanctification of this world. To some religions life in this world is valuable *solely because of* its limitations with regard to truthfulness and ultimacy. The non-ritualistic religion of later Judaism, for example sees truth as transcendent only, and the reality of life as essentially outside life, to be reached only after life, or in spite of life – that is, in spite of life as it is lived in this world. Time, in non-sacramental religions, is de-sanctified.

We cannot, however, simply say that the eschatological hope is the enemy of immanent truth and immediate salvation; for this is only so when the hope subsists expressly at the expense of the real presence or immediate availability of what is hoped for. The rite, be it remembered, holds within itself both time-lessness *and* time. We have seen how it sanctifies present time, and by doing so gives value to both past and future by its effect upon, due to its presence within, time as a whole, time as a dimension. Indeed, the role of myth in sacramental religion is to give explicit direction to the general ratification of history and time, to direct attention to specific events in time. The Christian Eucharist, for example, contains within it the eschatological hope in the very presence of that hope's immediate or real fulfilment, so that past and future – the creation of the world, the great feast at the world's end, the beginning of history and its consummation – turn around a centre or core of timelessness; or, better still, balance upon a fulcrum of timeless time – the time when time and eternity fuse, the history of Christ's Incarnate Life and Saving Acts.

Ritual faces both ways; it links two truths, two orders of experience. It is this Janus-quality in which the true character of the rite subsists. This world of experience is left behind so that it may be re-entered, re-experienced, restored. And so, not only is time established by ritual, but the entire human environment is blessed by its contact with – or rather its sojourn in – an ultimate dimension, a dimension which is believed to be the original source of all blessing. Ritual is an endorsement of the world, not an escape from it or a rejection of it. The world is left precisely in order for it to be re-entered.

The rite is thus a demonstration of the terms of relation between two orders – that the relationship is a true and valid one. Although the ritual order, the ritual time, is of so much greater value than the order it temporarily supplants, it is nevertheless in communication with that 'inferior' order, to such an extent that the latter can no longer be considered inferior in any pejorative sense of the word, so infused is it now with value and meaning as a partner in a 'two-way' traffic with the infinite.

Ritual belongs to both eternity and time, to *here* and to *there*, near and far, impossibility and the possible, truth about the immediate situation, and ultimate reality and Infinite Being. But it must be repeated the effect is never to distract, but always to establish – to make here-ness more here, and now-ness more now. The rite is not diffuseness but concentration. It is the moment of truth, in which all things, in heaven and earth, all that exists and all that *is*, conjoin. That is what the rite is in *essence*. It is always, therefore, in a real and profound sense a 'sacrament of unity'. This holds true of all cultures and every religion which possesses a cultus. Its immediate function is a practical one, to provide the means of existence, food for the journey through life; the journey *into* life. But this journey is no solitary one. This food is common food, however strange and exotic it may in one sense be. It is a food that all may eat, that all *must* eat. As the symbol of an ideal interaction and belonging, ritual takes the form of social communication, communication about society – although not necessarily or even primarily intellectual communication. The learning rituals of Lorenz's jackdaws do not merely embody what cannot be said by the birds, they embody what is better demonstrated than said in any society or family group.

All our ancient Christian rituals acknowledge the goodness of the natural order, the goodness of death. And yet, there seems so often to be very little substance in all this. If Western society once possessed this knowledge, it seems to have somehow forgotten about it. Indeed, in a very real sense, Western society has lost its roots. In our society, if not in our theology, death is 'homologised with the idea of Nothing' (Eliade). But we have reason to believe that if we could find a way of living more honestly – that is, closer to our natural selves, more in accordance with certain basic instincts and desires, certain natural movements of the spirit within us – then this terror of death as an emptiness of all value and meaning, death as simple uselessness and nothingness, would cease to oppress us. Are we to accept that these fears are unavoidable, that they are a basic human experience – the expression, in fact, of a primal 'death instinct' – that no movement on man's part can conquer them? Are we to see religion as an escape, a way of quitting human nature *and human society* altogether? Or is there a spiritual gesture which men are capable of, which belongs to men, which emerges from these fears, and is the existential answer to them, the natural human cure for them? Our response to God (to the Christian God, the transcendent God who is Spirit; Calvin's God as well as St Thomas's) is a human one. The movement of response is humanly made, according to human spirit. The human movement of response *also* heals. We might note that the statistics for neurosis among so-called primitive peoples in Africa and elsewhere lend support to the idea of an alienation and a negativity which are the invention of twentieth-century 'civilised' man, and which belong to the possibility of non-commitment, the option of 'living life on the sidelines' without ever becoming a real part of a community and fully sharing its corporate life, its vital structure of support and demand. The non-Christian African is more aware than we are of 'the things that belong to his peace'. So much is fact, and we know it. How is it we are unable to translate our knowledge into behaviour, to live our Christian insight as part of our actual daily experience of other people and of the world – that despite Our Lord's command we cannot 'set our troubled hearts at rest and banish our fears'?

The truth is, that theological statements and repetitions of the Creed are not enough to give us the mastery over our fears. It is not enough to learn about death and resurrection, or even to enact a dying and rising again which is merely an imitation of reality, and goes through the motions without feeling anything and certainly without changing anything. We must somehow manage to do the real thing. We must really die. We must really find new life. This is the primal force of our liturgy, surprising – or even shocking – as it may seem. But this, and no other, is the ritual inheritance that Christians share, that they share with all humanity. They have a Divine ratification of their impulse towards real rites of human solidarity, solidarity with one another and with their Incarnate Lord. They are aware in their rituals that they are redeemed not against their human experiences and aspirations but in them and through them.

The rite itself is human in that it is a structure of the religious consciousness. But it is human self-awareness, not human blindness. It is the human 'Thou' open to the 'Thou' of Otherness.

In the rite, man is lifted within a dimension of Being, into a time of wholeness, fullness, perfection. Whatever is made plain to him in that time may appear to belong to the world he sees, to 'this' world, or it may transcend it as surely as he himself transcends his former state. He is temporarily changed, the world is changed. Things are as they should be, and men 'may approach the gods as equals', or draw near the God of Heaven as beloved Sons, according to whether their intentions are towards the being of this world, or the One who transcends all earthly being. In itself, ritual is ours, it is our mode of responsive movement towards the Other; its purpose is to express human being as it should be, its function to enable it to be as it should be – as it knows it should be – that is, in love and relatedness. It is the affirmation of our understanding, our acknowledgement of the truth. As far as we are concerned it represents the utmost that we can do. We can only open ourselves, only proclaim and demonstrate our eagerness to receive, our need to receive, our willingness to give, our need to give. Openness to others is also openness to the Other. Our openness to other people, our awareness of relation, the ritual living of relationship, is the place and time of our meeting with God.

Bibliography

CHAPTER I

1. K. Bliss, *The Future of Religion*, Watts, 1969.
2. C. Levi-Strauss, *Totemism*, Penguin, 1969.
3. E. E. Evans-Pritchard, *Social Anthropology*, Routledge, 1951.
4. M. Douglas, *Purity and Danger*, Routledge, 1966.
5. S. Freud, *Obsessive Acts and Religious Practices*, Institute of Psychoanalysis Press, 1924.
   The Future of an Illusion, Hogarth Press, 1955.
   Totem and Taboo, Penguin, 1938.
   An Outline of Psychoanalysis, Hogarth Press, 1949.
6. R. Robinson (Ed.), *Readings in the Sociology of Religion*, Penguin, 1969.
7. M. Eliade, *Rites and Symbols of Initiation*, Harper, 1958.
   Patterns in Comparative Religion, Sheed & Ward, 1958.
   Myths, Dreams & Mysteries, Collins, 1968.
8. R. Graves, *The Greek Myths*, Penguin, 1955.
9. L. Bouyer, *Rite and Man*, Burns Oates, 1963.
10. A. van Gennep, *The Rites of Passage*, Routledge, 1960. (Ed. S. Kimball.)

CHAPTER 2

1. E. Bevan, *Symbolism and Belief* (Gifford Lectures, 1933), Collins, 1962.
2. K. Barth, *The Epistle to the Romans*, Oxford, 1929.
3. K. Heim, *Christian Faith and Natural Science*, S.C.M., 1953.
4. R. Bultmann, *Existence and Faith*, Collins, 1964.
   Jesus Christ and Mythology, S.C.M., 1958.
   Jesus and the World, Collins, 1958.
   Primitive Christianity, S.C.M., 1956.
5. E. Underhill, *Worship*, Collins, 1936.
6. L. Bouyer, *Rite and Man*, Burns Oates, 1963.
7. S. Kierkegaard, *Either/Or*, Doubleday.
8. P. Tillich, *The Courage to Be*, Collins, 1952.
9. M. Douglas, 'The Contempt of Ritual', *New Society*, 31/3/66.
10. J. Robinson, *On Being the Church in the World*, S.C.M., 1960.
11. A. von Speyr, *The Word*, Collins, 1953.
12. S. Freud, *Obsessive Acts and Religious Practices*, 1907.
13. S. Freud, *The Future of an Illusion*, 1927.
14. S. Freud, *Totem and Taboo*, 1919.
15. O. H. Mowrer, *The New Group Therapy*, Van Nostrand, 1964.
16. R. D. Laing, *The Divided Self*, Penguin, 1965.
    The Politics of Experience and *The Bird of Paradise*, Penguin, 1967.
17. S. Jourard, *The Transparent Self*, Van Nostrand, 1967.
18. A. Maslow, *Towards a Psychology of Being*, Van Nostrand, 1962.
19. R. May, *Love and Will*, Collins, 1972.
20. P. Tournier, *Guilt and Grace*, Hodder and Stoughton, 1962.
21. F. Lake, *Clinical Psychology*, D.L.T., 1966.
22. E. Erickson, *Childhood and Society*, Penguin, 1950.
23. M. Douglas, *Purity and Danger*, Routledge, 1966.
24. M. Eliade, *Myths, Dreams and Mysteries*, Collins, 1968.
25. C. G. Jung, *Analytical Psychology*, Routledge, 1968.
26. J. Frazer, *The Golden Bough* (Abridged Ed.), Macmillan, 1922.
27. B. Malinowski, *Magic, Science and Religion*, Doubleday, 1954.
28. E. Durkheim, 'The Social Foundations of Religion', in Robertson, *The Sociology of Religion*, Penguin, 1969.
29. T. Parsons, *Essays on Sociological Theory*, The Free Press of Glencoe, 1949.
30. W. Robertson-Smith, *The Religion of the Semites*, 1889.
31. A. van Gennep, *The Rites of Passage*, Routledge, 1960.

Bibliography

32. M. Gluckman, *Essays on the Ritual of Social Relationships*, Manchester, 1962.
33. R. H. Pfeiffer, *Religion in the Old Testament*, A. and C. Black, 1952.
34. R. H. Pfeiffer, *Introduction to the Old Testament*, A. and C. Black, 1961.
35. H. H. Rowley, *The Faith of Israel*, S.C.M., 1956.
36. W. Eichrodt, *Theology of the Old Testament*, Vol. 1, S.C.M., 1960.
37. G. Lienhardt, 'Divinity and Experience', in Robertson, *The Sociology of Religion*, Penguin, 1969.

CHAPTER 3

1. A. Artaud, *The Theatre and Its Double*, Calder & Boyars, 1970.
2. D. Winzen, *Symbols of Christ*, Longmans, 1957.
3. M. Eliade, *Rites and Symbols of Initiation*, Harper and Row, 1958.
4. M. Douglas, *Purity and Danger*, Routledge, 1966.
5. A. van Gennep, *The Rites of Passage*, Routledge, 1960.
6. A. J. Ungersma, *The Search for Meaning*, Allen & Unwin, 1961.
7. M. Buber, *Between Man and Man*, Collins, 1947.
8. E. Fromm, *The Sane Society*, Routledge, 1956.
9. G. Marcel, *Being and Having*, Collins, 1965.
10. J. P. Sartre, *Being and Nothingness*, Methuen, 1969.
11. S. Freud, *An Outline of Psychoanalysis*, Hogarth Press, 1949.
12. A. Camus, *The Myth of Sisyphus*, H. Hamilton, 1955.
13. D. von Hildebrand, *Liturgy and Personality*, Longmans, 1943.
14. M. Eliade, *Myths, Dreams and Mysteries*, Collins, 1968.
15. G. Dix, *The Shape of the Liturgy*, Dacre, 1947.
16. O Cullmann, *Early Christian Worship*, S.C.M., 1953.
17. A. Maslow, *Towards a Psychology of Being*, Van Nostrand, 1962.

CHAPTER 4

1. M. Eliade, *Patterns of Comparative Religion*, Sheed & Ward, 1958.
2. M. Picard, *The World of Silence*.
3. E. Fromm, *The Sane Society*, Routledge, 1956.
4. R. May, *Love and Will*, Collins, 1972.
5. R. D. Laing, *The Politics of Experience*, Penguin, 1969.

The Language of the Rite

6. D. Sayers, *Unpopular Opinions*, Gollancz, 1940.
7. S. Kierkegaard, *Crisis in the Life of an Actress*, Collins, 1967.
8. S. H. Butcher, *Commentary on Arisotle's 'Poatics'*, Dover, 1951.
9. F. Hegel, *Lectures on Aesthetics, Selected Writings*, Collins, 1964.
10. M. Buber, *I and Thou*, T. and T. Clark, 1958.
11. G. Marcel, *Being and Having*, Collins, 1965.
12. M. Buber, *Pointing the Way*, Routledge, 1957.
13. L. Bouyer, *Rite and Man*, Burns Oates, 1963.
14. A. Artaud, *The Theatre and its Double*, Calder & Boyars, 1970.
15. A. van Gennep, *The Rites of Passage*, Routledge, 1965
16. W. Eichrodt, *Theology of the Old Testament*, S.C.M., 1960.

176